# FROM HANDSHAKE TO CLOSING
# The Role of the Commercial Real Estate Lawyer

Sidney G. Saltz

Defending Liberty
Pursuing Justice

**Real Property, Trust and Estate Law**
**Media/Books Products Committee**
Candace M. Cunningham, *Editor-in-Chief*
Phyllis M. Rubinstein, *Editor-in-Chief Emeritus*
Aen Walker Webster, *Editor-in-Chief Emeritus*

**Real Property**
Christopher B. Hanback, *Managing Editor*
Richard Frome, *Acquisitions Editor*
Scott S. Shepardson, *Acquisitions Editor*
Amy McShane, *Acquisitions. Editor*
Megan Ballard, *Books Editor*
Cynthia Boyer Blakeslee, *Books Editor*
Michael A. DiOrio, *Book Editor*

**Trust and Estate**
Carolyn P. Vinson, *Managing Editor*
William A. Drennan, *Series Editor*
Michael G. Goldstein, *Series Editor*
Michael A. Kirtland, *Acquisitions Editor*
Elizabeth Lindsay-Ochoa, *Acquisitions Editor*
Suzanne Luna, *Acquisitions Editor*
Harry Pskowski, *Acquisitions Editor*
Michael Speilman, *Acquisitions Editor*
Doug L. Siegler, *Acquisitions/Marketing Editor*
Nancy E. Shurtz, *Senior Books Editor*

Cover design by ABA Publishing.

The materials contained herein represent the opinions of the authors and editors and should not be construed to be the action of either the American Bar Association or the Section of Real Property, Trust and Estate Law unless adopted pursuant to the bylaws of the Association.

Nothing contained in this book is to be considered as the rendering of legal advice for specific cases, and readers are responsible for obtaining such advice from their own legal counsel. This book and any forms and agreements herein are intended for educational and informational purposes only.

No part of this publication may be reproduced, stored in a retrieval system, or transmitted in any form or by any means, electronic, mechanical, photocopying, recording, or otherwise, without the prior written permission of the publisher. For permission contact the ABA Copyrights & Contracts Department, copyright@abanet.org or via fax at 312 988-6030.

© 2008 American Bar Association. All rights reserved. Printed in the United States of America.

Library of Congress Cataloging-in-Publication Data

From handshake to closing : the role of the commercial real estate lawyer / Sidney G. Saltz, editor.
   p. cm.
  Includes index.
  ISBN 978-1-59031-961-1
  1. Vendors and purchasers--United States. 2. Real property--United States. I. Saltz, Sidney G.

KF665.F76 2008
346.7304'37--dc22
                                        2007049835

07 06 05 04 03   5 4 3 2 1

Discounts are available for books ordered in bulk. Special consideration is given to state bars, CLE programs, and other bar-related organizations. Inquire at ABA Publishing, American Bar Association, 321 N. Clark Street, Chicago IL 60610. Visit us at www.ababooks.org

# Table of Contents

*Acknowledgments* .................................................................... v

*Preface* ............................................................................. vii

**Introduction: The Lawyer's Role** ...................................... 1

**Enter the Broker** ............................................................... 5

**Pre-Documentation Documents** ........................................ 9

    Letters of Intent .................................................................. 9
    Loan Commitments ........................................................... 13

**Documenting the Transaction** ......................................... 17

    Who Will Draft? ................................................................ 17
    Forms ................................................................................. 19
    The Functions of Drafting ................................................. 23
    Drafting for Clarity; Drafting for Readability ................... 25
    The Case of the Proliferating Adjectives .......................... 32
    Dispute Resolution ............................................................ 32
    Vagueness .......................................................................... 33
    Some Substantive Provisions ............................................ 37
    Boilerplate ......................................................................... 49
    A Final Word .................................................................... 50
    Conclusion ......................................................................... 50

**Reviewing and Analyzing Documents** ............................ 51

    Examples ........................................................................... 53
    Matters Not Covered in the Document under Review ..... 71
    External Factors ................................................................ 72
    Now What? ........................................................................ 73
    Subleases ........................................................................... 74
    Ground Leases .................................................................. 75
    Conduit Mortgages ............................................................ 77
    Conclusion ......................................................................... 77

**Negotiating** ............................................................................... 79

    Communicating Your Response ............................................. 79
    Preparation ................................................................................ 85
    The Negotiation ........................................................................ 90
    A Scenario ................................................................................ 93
    A Lease Issue—Insurance ........................................................ 96
    A Contentious Contract Issue—Warranties ............................ 96
    Generalizing from the Particular ........................................... 100
    Mistakes ................................................................................. 102
    Conclusion ............................................................................. 103

**Finishing Up** ........................................................................... 105

**What Else?** .............................................................................. 109

    Title and Survey .................................................................... 113
    Other Due Diligence Issues ................................................... 117

**Preparing for Closing** ............................................................ 119

**Closing** .................................................................................... 123

**Conclusion** .............................................................................. 125

# Acknowledgments

I gratefully acknowledge the assistance of the people who read this manuscript and provided invaluable advice, particularly Milton Podolsky and my colleague Philip Wong.

# Preface

Who am I and why am I writing this book?

I am a lawyer, practicing general real estate law. I have been doing so for about 40 years. After graduating from Northwestern University in 1959, where I majored in political science, I attended Yale Law School, where I received my LLB in 1962. I joined Jenner & Block, then the sixth largest law firm in Chicago, but left for a one year clerkship with the Chief Judge of the United States Court of Appeals for the Second Circuit in New York. I returned to Jenner & Block, practiced in the area of antitrust and general litigation for three years, after which I moved into real estate law, which I have been doing ever since, with Jenner until 1999, with Barnes & Thornburg through 2005, and now with Holland & Knight.

That autobiographical material is important for several reasons. First, it shows that, although I received a fine education, I was not a business or accounting major. I went right from undergraduate school to law school, and then into practice, clerked, and back into practice again. I do not have the training or experience in business to enable me to evaluate the potential benefits or detriments of a transaction. That is both a curse and a blessing: I am not in a position to consult with and advise the client on its business decisions, but neither do I try to substitute my judgment for the client's or try to affect the progress of a deal because of a difference of opinion with the client. Rather, I view my role as the legal advisor, bringing to bear my experience and my own *legal* expertise to assist the client in making decisions.

Second, I have spent time clerking and litigating. Although my experience litigating is not extensive, it does afford me some insight on how disputes may arise and why it is so important to avoid them.

Third, I have been practicing law for a long time. That is not necessarily something to be proud of; every transaction lawyer (who survives, that is) gets older, works for many years and witnesses many changes—some good and some not so good. During that period of time, one does learn something, often from one's own mistakes, but usually from other people or from simply doing and thinking—using the base of experience to improve one's own skills and the tools used in one's work. That brings us to the question of why I am spending my time writing this book. No doubt, doing is a better teacher than reading. Mentoring is better than reading. On the other hand, I have seen the practice of real estate law become much more complex over the years, and I have witnessed a change in the way in which law firms, particularly large law firms, now handle the training of young people. With their high fees and an emphasis on billable hours, they often thrust complicated matters upon young lawyers and force them to learn through trial and error. When I started practicing in the real estate field, the law was much simpler and the documentation was much less extensive. Many of the laws and regulations that are now an unavoidable part of practice did not exist; there was no environmental regulation, no Americans with Disabilities Act, and no Real Estate Settlement Procedures Act, just to cite three examples. To close a residential deal in Illinois in 1966, you needed four documents: a deed, a bill of sale, an affidavit of title, and a closing statement. The loan documents usually consisted of a note and mortgage, and the closing took place at the lender's or the lawyer's office. The documents required to close a loan on a warehouse building consisted of the note, mortgage, assignment of rents and leases, usury affidavit, title, and survey. If it was a construction loan, there would be a construction loan agreement as well. The closing binder was half an inch thick. How thick are they today?

Years ago, lawyers were trained in ways that are really unavailable today. Notwithstanding the fact that, in more leisurely times, young lawyers used to be taken to meetings and closings so they could observe and learn—without billing the client for their time—there were other opportunities to learn that are now lost. For example, in the days before title companies did ownership searches, and before there were paralegals, young lawyers would go to the recorder's office or the title company and look things up in tract books. I assume that most young lawyers practicing real estate law today do not even know what a tract book is. All deeds, easements, subdivisions, and anything else recorded against real estate were logged by hand into large books. Anyone could check to see which tract books related to the property he or she was interested in knowing about, order those books, and page through them. Once one found a document number, he or she could go to the recorder's office and view the copy of the document, sometimes in white print on a black background and at other times in old books in which the documents were actually hand copied (in the most beautiful and flawless handwriting, incidentally). Admittedly, the old system was not as efficient as ordering an ownership search and getting copies of the documents from a title company, but the experience gave the young lawyer something tangible, a feeling for what legal descriptions meant, how properties were divided and conveyed, and how conveyances or encumbrances were recorded and indexed. We learned what sections and ranges and meridians were and how they looked on maps. Sometimes closings occurred in the Torrens Office, and the county provided a form of registration of title and issued duplicate certificates of title, just as secretaries of state issue automobile titles (that was an experience!). Perhaps I am just being nostalgic, but still I sense that the fact that those hands-on experiences are no longer available means that younger practitioners are missing something useful. Certainly, it is possible to become an able real estate lawyer without those experiences, but I cannot help feeling that they were valuable for me.

It is my intention and my hope that this book will assist lawyers in avoiding those pitfalls that condemn them to be what all clients (and particularly their brokers) consider the worst kind of lawyer—the DEAL KILLER. To do that, I will give some suggestions on how to handle the various stages of a deal, and to add a little flavor to this book (for my entertainment as well as yours), I will continue to provide some history of the practice through examples—war stories, if you will—of situations I have encountered in my career. The reader is, of course, free to skip those if he or she desires. I will not know, so I will not be insulted.

# Introduction: The Lawyer's Role

Not every deal should be made, and not every deal should be closed.

That may seem a strange way to begin a book about closing deals, but it is true. So what is the lawyer's role in the decision as to whether to proceed with a particular deal? As I explained in the Preface, I do not have the business training necessary to advise clients on such a question. What I do have, however, is some experience documenting and closing deals and, I hope, some common sense and street-smarts, gleaned from years of experience. Still, it is not for the lawyer to veto a deal the client wants to make. It is appropriate for a lawyer, especially one with business sense, to advise the client on the pitfalls of a particular deal, but the decision must remain with the client. It is, after all, the client's money, not the lawyer's, which is at risk. If the deal is not a good one, it is the client, not the lawyer, who will lie awake at night.[1] If proceeding with the transaction might expose the client to litigation or possible liability, the lawyer must advise the client, at least to protect him- or herself from professional liability. If the client is proposing to do something which violates the law, the lawyer certainly has the obligation to advise against it and, if the client persists, to withdraw rather than to aid and abet the activity. Short of that situation, interference is a certain way to lose a client.

However, if the deal is bad enough, you may lose the client anyway. My former partner represented two young men who were buying a troubled shopping center. They negotiated a securitized

---

[1] The situation may be different if the lawyer partners with, or even invests with, the client. In the case of a partnership, the lawyer is his own client and his judgment, in his capacity as lawyer, may well be compromised. Even if the lawyer is a limited partner or is not directly involved in the decisions of the entity, his judgment may be affected by his investment. I will, however, not deal extensively with the legal and ethical problems inherent in those situations.

loan,[2] which my partner and I realized was unwise because the transaction costs would be much too high and the loan was not appropriate under the circumstances. The clients were fixated on the interest rate, however, and that was all they cared about so they did the deal. We also warned them that, under its terms, the loan could not be prepaid for some time, and that it would then have to be "defeased", i.e., they would have to post government securities to provide for the continuation of the stream of payments for the investors (the equivalent of a large prepayment penalty). We later found out that they intended all along to resell the property (which they never told us) and were shocked when they could not do so. They probably did not pay the entire legal fee and they certainly did not use our services again—just as well.

When it comes to documenting and negotiating the deal the lawyer's advice becomes more appropriate. At this stage, the lawyer has two major concerns: first, that the deal agreed to between the parties is actually incorporated into the documents, and second, that the documents do not contain provisions that impose unacceptable risks on the client. It is also at this stage of the transaction that the lawyer has the most power to kill a deal, and the most influence over his or her client because the lawyer likely will have greater expertise.[3]

In this connection, it should be borne in mind that there is a material difference between deals relating to the purchase and sale of real estate, and those involving leases or mortgages. The principal difference is that purchases and sales, other than installment sales, generally close within a reasonably brief period of time. The parties and the lawyers need not concern themselves with what might happen three or five years down the road. Yes, there are warranties and indemnities in those agreements, but they generally speak of events that occurred before the closing and often will become known within a relatively brief time span. If a problem is

---

[2] Securitized loans will be discussed more fully below.
[3] A situation of concern may arise if the client is also a lawyer or, to put it another way, has a law degree. If that client has not practiced in the lawyer's field, he or she may have less expertise than he or she believes. Inappropriate second guessing may occur and that could be a major problem for the lawyer. Thankfully, I have found this situation to be rare, but it does occur.

## Introduction: The Lawyer's Role

discovered during due diligence, or a fire or condemnation occurs, either the parties will work it out under the terms of the contract, or the deal will not close. Of course, the drafters of the contract must provide for those contingencies, but they typically are not great sticking points during the negotiations.

On the other hand, the rights and obligations of the parties to a lease, a mortgage, or even an installment contract continue for years, during which time many unexpected things may happen. In the lease situation, for example, the method of taxation may change, the building may have a fire, the tenant may go bankrupt or otherwise default, and the tenant's use may damage the premises in some unanticipated way, the tenant may outgrow the space or its business may shrink, making the premises inappropriate for its use. Chances are those things will not occur, but they may. Contingencies must be anticipated and provided for. The same is true for mortgages, which typically go on for at least five or ten years. What is to happen, for example, if the tenant, on whose rent the loan was predicated, defaults, abandons the property, or goes bankrupt? Who will receive the proceeds of fire insurance? Who contests the award if a condemnation occurs?

The evaluation of the other party to the transaction and its credit is essentially the responsibility of your client and his or her broker, if there is one. On the other hand, it is not inappropriate for the lawyer to remind the client to review financial statements and to confirm that the entity with which it is dealing is the appropriate one from a financial standpoint. Certainly, if the other party is a corporation or other entity registered with a state, it is the lawyer's duty to determine that the entity exists and is in good standing.

Whose job is it to think of everything bad that could happen and to protect against those contingencies? The lawyer, of course. And woe unto that lawyer who thinks of everything that could happen, except the one thing that actually happens.

It is important to remember that the lawyers documenting, reviewing, and negotiating the transaction are also creating the law of the transaction. Except for the proscriptions imposed by public policy (as reflected in court decisions and legislation) and the concept of good faith and fair dealing, the parties are freely able to determine, by their documents, how their agreement is to be implemented and disputes resolved. This makes the persons involved extremely powerful, but power also demands responsibility.

In this book, I will discuss the role of the broker, letters of intent, the problems inherent in documenting deals, and how to review documents, communicate comments, negotiate deals, conduct due diligence, prepare for closing, and conduct the closing itself.

# Enter the Broker

Many deals involve the services of brokers. Some deals that do not involve brokers should. This is especially true when the client is a tenant or a user, rather than a developer or investor in real estate, and does not know the market or understand how real estate deals are done. A good broker knows the market and has a sense of what business terms should be negotiated in a given situation. In other words, he or she provides the business and financial information to the client that the client might otherwise expect the lawyer to provide, and that generally is outside the lawyer's area of expertise.

When I am contacted by a client, or referred a matter by another lawyer in my office, and the client is not sophisticated in real estate transactions, the first question I ask is whether he or she is represented by a broker. If the answer is no, then my next question is whether the client is confident that the deal is a good one. Often, the answer I get is not encouraging. In those cases, I suggest that the client consult with a broker, and I advise the client that it may still be possible for the broker to be paid a commission by the landlord or seller, as the case may be.

I like brokers and have many friends who are in that line of work. Some of my clients are brokers as well as property owners, and my wife is a commercial real estate broker. I have had many referrals from brokers, and sometimes I work only with the broker in connection with a matter and never even meet or speak with the client. In those situations, the client obviously has sufficient confidence in the broker as well, so that he or she does not feel it necessary to deal directly with me.

Despite my own comfort level with brokers, I am well aware that there is a great deal of mutual suspicion between the brokerage and the legal communities. Much of the problem arises out of the way brokers and lawyers customarily are compensated. Whereas lawyers generally are paid on an hourly basis, brokers

*From Handshake to Closing*

usually are paid commissions. Hence, brokers tend to be more entrepreneurial and lawyers tend to be more conservative. The broker's role often is perceived by lawyers as one seeking compromise over disputed items so that the deal may be concluded, and the lawyer's role generally is perceived by brokers as one steering his client away from risk. Brokers often view lawyers as deal killers.

Like all general perceptions, those may have some truth. Of course, there are brokers who put the parties together and disappear, leaving the parties and their lawyers to finish the deal. There are other brokers who stay involved, but do not read the contract or lease, have no knowledge of the issues inherent in those documents, and contribute nothing to the negotiation. Finally, there are brokers who are knowledgeable about the documents, read them, and contribute to the negotiations. Those are the brokers who truly represent their client's interests, in effect put those interests ahead of their own, and recognize that it is better to retain the client and be able to move on to another deal or a referral than to take the commission and leave the client holding the bag.

Another issue between lawyers and brokers is that lawyers suspect, and it is often the case that brokers are drafting documents that are really within the purview of the practice of law. What constitutes the practice of law or, more to the point, the unauthorized practice of law, is a hot issue and creates certain hostility between the two professions. On numerous occasions, I lectured about leases in courses offered to brokers with a broker client, Steven H. Podolsky.[4] We would ask how many of the brokers drafted lease language. Many hands always went up. When we explained that, when lease language is ambiguous, courts frequently resort to the rule of construction that provides that a document is construed most strongly against the drafter, and if the broker drafted ambiguous language and his or her client lost a lawsuit construing that language, the broker's errors and omissions insurance would not cover the situation because it does not cover the unauthorized practice of law by brokers, I think we put enough concern in those bro-

---

[4] I acknowledge that many of the ideas presented in this section, as well as in other sections of this book, were learned from Steve, for which I express my gratitude.

kers' minds that many of them no longer drafted lease language. Of course, the same principle applies to contracts.[5]

Many, perhaps most, lawyers do not consult the broker involved in the deal. Those lawyers have only a partial, possibly distorted view of the transaction. The broker will have worked with the client, perhaps for months, and will know, intimately, the goals and objectives of the client, whereas the lawyer may be called in only after the deal is cut, and be confronted with documentation which may or may not reflect the client's desires. The lawyer may find many objectionable provisions in the documents, but be wholly unaware that the client or the other party has some peculiar issues that make the client's bargaining position either particularly strong or particularly weak. The broker is much more likely to know those facts than the lawyer. If the lawyer is focusing only on the documents and not on the goals and objectives of his or her client, or on the bargaining position of the parties, the lawyer is doing the client a grave disservice.

In addition, document review and negotiation may take a long time. Sometimes it is because the lawyer is busy and cannot get to the matter right away, but on other occasions, the delay is a result of the length of the document and the necessity to give it a very careful review. The negotiations may be protracted, since it may take some time to reach a meeting of the minds on issues one or the other lawyer deems important. Brokers generally want to get the deal done quickly, which is perfectly understandable. It is not unusual for the broker to give a sense of urgency to the matter, and to press the lawyer to be prompt and diligent in his or her review and negotiation. This can sometimes be disconcerting to the busy lawyer, but it does help get deals done promptly.

For all these reasons, a good broker can save the lawyer from terrible embarrassment, or worse.

Representing a client in any transaction is a team effort. It involves the efforts not only of the lawyer and broker, but also many other professionals, depending, of course, on the transaction. They may include the insurance agent, the architect, the contractor, the environmental engineer, the roofer, the structural engineer, the

---

[5] More about that rule of construction later.

tax consultant, and many others. Many brokers believe they should be the leader of the team, and often they have a legitimate right to that belief, but it is irrelevant who the leader is. If it is truly a team effort, the parties should work together to achieve the real objective, which is to serve the client's interest.

Although lawyers and brokers "make decisions" as to various matters, the ultimate decision maker is the client. It is, after all, the client's money. The role of all the professionals involved in the deal is to seek to narrow the issues and to present open issues to the client for decision. Each decision must be an informed one, based on sound advice. The lawyer and broker should strive for a meeting of the minds on their recommendations to the client, but if they cannot agree, they can each present their points of view as dispassionately as possible so that the client understands the alternatives and can make the decision.

The relationship between the lawyer and broker can be an excellent learning experience for each. A young lawyer can learn a great deal from an able and experienced broker, and lawyers have, in my opinion, a responsibility to help educate brokers about the intricacies of the legal documents involved. If the lawyer does so, he or she may find a grateful partner in many transactions referred to the lawyer by that broker.

In sum, the lawyer should approach his or her dealings with brokers openly and assume, until proven otherwise, that the broker is ethical and is as concerned as the lawyer about getting a good and fair deal for the client. If proved wrong, the lawyer must then work to protect the client from the broker in addition to the people on the other side of the deal.

# Pre-Documentation Documents

Before getting into the documentation of the deal, the parties often negotiate the terms of the transaction, which are then memorialized in some sort of written document. It may be a term sheet or a letter of intent, or in the case of a mortgage loan, a loan commitment. Term sheets or letters of intent (which I will refer to simply as "letters of intent") are generally not intended to be binding on the parties. On the other hand, a loan commitment is a contract between the lender and the borrower and its terms are enforceable. First, I shall discuss letters of intent.

## Letters of Intent

The first question to be considered is, "When are letters of intent binding?" That leads to the next question, which is, "For what purpose?" Are they binding for the purpose of creating an obligation to negotiate in good faith? Or are they binding as an agreement between the parties?

    I do not propose to discuss the many cases on letters of intent which deal with those issues—for that, I commend to you an excellent article by Thomas C. Homburger and James R. Schuller entitled *Letters of Intent—A Trap for the Unwary*.[6] In that article, the authors determined that, depending on the jurisdiction, the answer may turn partly on the drafting of the letter of intent and partly on other evidence of the intent of the parties. In other words, even though there may be language in a letter of intent stating that it is not intended to bind the parties to an agreement until a final agreement is written up, executed and delivered, the parties may in fact be bound. At the very least, a letter of intent may create an obligation to negotiate in good faith.

---

[6] 37 REAL PROPERTY, PROBATE & TRUST J. 509 (Fall 2002).

Brokers like letters of intent. First, but not necessarily foremost, the letter of intent may result in the entitlement to a commission, based on the broker having found a "ready, willing, and able" tenant or purchaser for his or her client's space. More often, however, commissions are not really earned until a lease is signed or the sale is closed, so we should not impute negative motives to brokers. No, brokers like letters of intent because they document the basic terms of the deal and facilitate the drafting of the lease or contract document. Usually, letters of intent drafted by brokers contain language which negates the intent to create a binding agreement, but as noted above, it may not be entirely effective. Often, a broker representing a tenant will make a "request for proposal" (an RFP) to the landlord or its broker and receive a detailed response which will contain the business terms of the deal. Sometimes, the broker representing the tenant or buyer will make an "offer", setting forth the terms on which the tenant is willing to enter into the lease or the buyer is willing to enter into a contract. That offer may be "accepted" or may be subject to a "counteroffer". I put the words in quotation marks because the offers, acceptances and counteroffers are not really intended to be used in the context of creating a binding agreement, and they probably do not do so for several reasons. First, it is understood in the trade that it is not their purpose. More importantly, the broker does not usually have the authority to bind his client to a lease or contract. The actual parties do not customarily sign the papers being exchanged (unless, of course, there are no brokers involved). The problem really arises when the brokers take the terms that have been discussed, either orally or by RFP or offer and acceptance, and reduce them to writing in a letter of intent and ask the parties to sign them. Remember that at this point it is most likely that neither party has consulted its attorney.

Let us assume that I am consulted at that point in the process. Whether I represent the landlord or the tenant, or the buyer or the seller, my advice is, "Don't sign!" The parties, by signing may create a binding agreement, even though important matters have not been dealt with, or have been dealt with in an imprecise manner. Even if the letter of intent is accurate and contains all sorts of language about not creating a binding lease, there may still be

## Pre-Documentation Documents

problems. The problems may be made worse by making the letter of intent very detailed. I have seen letters of intent which were extremely long and contained almost all of the terms of the agreement, using in many instances, the very language of a lease or contract. I do not believe that any amount of language which states that the letter of intent is not binding (except, perhaps, conditions like board approval) could have kept that letter of intent from actually being enforced as the agreement between the parties.

What are some of the other problems with letters of intent? Although a major purpose of a letter of intent is to discourage each party from seeking a better deal before the current negotiations are wrapped up, some letters of intent actually require the landlord or seller to cease marketing the property. In representing a landlord or seller, I strongly object to that provision (if I see it in advance) because it places what I deem to be intolerable burdens on that party. It may have to incur the cost of removing large and expensive "For Sale" or "For Rent" signs (and replacing them if the deal does not go through), but that is a minor matter compared to the requirement that the client turn away prospects when it does not have a firm deal. The problem is more serious in a sale situation than in the lease situation, because not only will the negotiation of the contract take time but the buyer probably will probably be afforded a period of time to conduct its due diligence, at the end of which it may terminate the contract for any reason or no reason at all, leaving the seller with the property and no alternative prospects.

Secondly, the letter of intent may create an obligation to negotiate in good faith, and the refusal to agree to some important term may result in a claim (and litigation) that the party has failed to live up to that obligation. That puts particular pressure on the parties subsequently negotiating the lease or contract, especially if, in the course of negotiation, issues are raised (and agreed to) that are inconsistent with the terms of the letter of intent.

I experienced an example of that some years ago. A landlord client signed a letter of intent which committed the landlord to forego certain additional rent pass-throughs.[7] The tenant asked for more build-out than was contemplated by the landlord (the issue

---

[7] "Pass-through" is shorthand for additional rent based on taxes and operating expenses incurred by the landlord in connection with the property.

*From Handshake to Closing*

was not clear in the letter of intent). The landlord granted the concession, but changed the lease to restore the pass-throughs and sent a red-lined copy of the lease to the tenant, highlighting the change in the pass-throughs. The tenant signed the red-lined copy of the lease and then sued the landlord, claiming that the lease did not accurately reflect the agreement of the parties. To avoid protracted litigation and expense, the landlord settled the case. Under the circumstances, what do I recommend?

1. The parties should not sign letters of intent. I mean that in two senses. The parties should avoid using letters of intent, but if they do use them, they should not sign them. There are alternative to letters of intent which are far less dangerous. For example, I recommend using a term sheet. It states, in essence, that "the following are the terms on which the parties propose to lease (or sell or purchase) such and such property" and then only the basic terms are set out. It is always wise to provide that it is not a binding agreement and to set out a date after which either party may terminate discussions without liability. It may even expressly negate an obligation to negotiate in good faith. Vagueness is the key. If the parties do not sign the letter of intent and the statute of frauds applies, the letter of intent does not bind the parties. There are two caveats. First, if a broker signs for a party, it should be clear that he is without authority to bind the party. Second, beware of the Federal Electronic Signatures Act. A letter of intent sent via e-mail by a person employed by the one of the parties who has authority to sign a lease may satisfy the requirements of that Act and bind the party.

2. If parties must use and sign a letter of intent, it should contain language negating the intent to create a binding agreement. If possible, conditions to the conclusion of a lease or contract should be inserted, such as board approval or tenant's or buyer's confirmation of the zoning or condition of the premises, in its discretion, or the landlord's satisfaction, again in its discretion, with the tenant's financial condition or its operation of its prior premises. If the obligation to negotiate in good faith is not to be negated, time periods

## Pre-Documentation Documents

should be provided for the delivery of the draft lease or contract and for the completion of the negotiations, after which time the parties will have no obligations under the letter of intent.

3. If you represent the landlord or seller, recommend to your client that it not agree to take the space off the market until a lease is signed or the sale is closed.

Unfortunately, it is unlikely that the lawyer will be consulted before a letter of intent is signed. To assure that he or she has a chance to review it, the lawyer must know that the deal is contemplated, that a broker has been hired, and that a deal is imminent. It will take a very close relationship with the client of the broker for the lawyer to have that kind of information.

## Loan Commitments

Usually, but not always, the lawyer knows that his or her client is seeking financing. That does not assure that the lawyer will be consulted before a loan commitment is signed. If the client is a real estate professional, he or she may be aware of the risks in signing a commitment without legal advice. At least that client will have had the opportunity to have learned from a bad experience. Where the borrower is a user of the property—a company which is acquiring or owns the property and is financing it for the conduct of its non-real estate business, he or she is not likely to know the risks of signing the commitment without first showing it to the lawyer. This is especially a problem when the commitment is not labeled a commitment at all, but a loan application which becomes a commitment when accepted. The client may think he or she has another bite at the apple, but in truth, he or she does not.

Any number of issues may come into play in connection with the loan application or commitment, which, of course, is drafted on the lender's form. First and foremost is the issue of recourse; is the borrower to have personal liability for the loan and if so, to what extent? If the lender's recourse for the payment of the debt is limited to its security (i.e. the foreclosure of the mortgage and the exercise of its rights under the assignment of leases and rents or the security agreement), what exclusions (generally referred to as "carve-outs") are there to be from the non-recourse nature of the loan? What are the matters for which the borrower or guarantor is to have personal liability? Another issue is that of a lock-in, i.e., a period of time during which the loan may not be prepaid. The application or commitment may also provide for a substantial prepayment penalty, or a "due on sale or transfer" clause, which requires prepayment if the property is transferred (sometimes with the prepayment penalty being due at that time). The death of one of the principals of the borrower may trigger such an event. All these and possibly other important business terms must be dealt with at the commitment or application stage, or the borrower will be bound by terms it may not even have considered or evaluated. Once the application or commitment is signed, there is very little a lawyer can do to negotiate those provisions when the loan documents are being reviewed.

There is one particular issue which I always consider, even if the subject is not dealt with in the commitment or application. I want to assure that, if there is a fire or other casualty, the insurance proceeds will be made available by the lender to restore the property. Why is that important?

Most mortgages provide that if there is a fire or other casualty, the insurance proceeds are to be paid to the lender. The lender may either apply the proceeds to the loan or make them available to the borrower to restore the property. Assume that there is a fire and part of the building is damaged or destroyed. If in that situation, the proceeds are applied to the loan balance, the amount of the debt will be reduced but, as a rule, the debt service payments will not. For example, if the loan was $1 million and the monthly payments were $10,000, and the insurance proceeds were $600,000, the loan balance would be reduced to $400,000, but the monthly payments would remain at $10,000. Further, if the borrower does not get the proceeds, it will not be in a position to rebuild and may lose its tenants, who provide the wherewithal to pay the debt service. The borrower may not even have the right to prepay the balance of the loan and refinance, which will essentially ruin him or her. That is why having the lender be obligated to make the proceeds available (with appropriate protections for the lender) is so critical.[8]

I had a situation once where the client owned an office complex of five buildings. He was financing one of them, and I tried to negotiate to have the commitment provide that the proceeds would be made available to rebuild. The lender refused. If that building had burned down, leaving the other four, and if it were not rebuilt because the insurance proceeds were not made available, the remaining buildings would not have been leaseable. Since the lender was adamant, the client had to find a different lender. If I had not negotiated that issue at the commitment stage, the client would either have been stuck with a bad loan, or would have had to breach the agreement contained in the commitment, with the loss of its commitment fee, and possibly a lawsuit.

The importance of legal input and negotiations at the commitment stage cannot be overestimated.

---

[8] I have considered the issue of the availability of the proceeds of casualty insurance in *Tug of War—Who Gets the Casualty Insurance Proceeds?*, PROBATE & PROPERTY (July/Aug. 1999), at 32.

# Documenting the Transaction

Okay. The preliminaries are over. We now have a pretty good idea of the basics of the deal. Now the deal has to be documented. This is, of course, a critical phase of the transaction, because what is now written down (or more likely, typed into the computer), after changes are made as a result of input from the client and its broker and negotiations with the other party and its lawyers and brokers are concluded, will form the blueprint of the transaction and will provide the basis for the resolution of any future disputes between the parties. It will, as noted above, become the "law" of the deal.

## Who Will Draft?

Who will do the drafting? That depends on the nature of the deal. If it is a mortgage, the lender may have standard form documents, or its lawyer will draft the loan documents. It is a manifestation of the "golden rule of lending" which holds that "Them what's got the gold makes the rules." One of those "rules" is that the lender's documents are used. Only once in my years of practice have I been asked, as the borrower's attorney, to draft the loan documents, and that was because the borrower had a special relationship with the bank and I had previously done many deals with that bank, on behalf of my client.

In the leasing situation, the document is generally drafted by the landlord's lawyer. In retail, where the store is located in a shopping center, however small, the landlord needs uniformity in its leases. It cannot, for example, have different definitions of common area expenses or different bases for collecting tax pass-throughs; it cannot have differing ways of handling losses by fire or casualty. It would be an administrative nightmare.[9] Similarly, in

---

[9] This does not mean that the provisions in the lease cannot be negotiated to some extent, because the payment provisions may be broader than what the landlord actually intends to collect. More about this later.

office leasing, the landlord needs to have common provisions so it does not have to review all of its leases to make decisions in connection with its management of the property. Even in the industrial or warehouse situation, landlord's need uniformity, especially if the properties are in an industrial park.

On the other hand, many tenants have their own lease forms and, especially if they lease many locations all over the region or all over the nation, they feel they need some uniformity for their own administration of their business. They, too, have a legitimate concern. In my experience, however, tenants' form leases do not take sufficient notice of matters which are of critical importance to landlords, and leases made on their forms may not, in fact be mortgageable (i.e., in determining the amount of the loan, a lender would not give credit for rent payable under that lease, even if the tenant has excellent credit). Provisions which give tenants set-offs against the rent or rights to terminate the lease for landlord's defaults are examples of matters which might negate the mortgagability of a lease.

I recently reviewed a lease form that a tenant submitted in connection with the leasing of a relatively small store. The tenant was a national tax preparation company (I will be discussing the role of the lawyer in reviewing documents prepared by their counterparts on the other side of the deal in greater detail below, but I want to use this example to illustrate the problems of tenant lease forms). It took me a long time to review the lease. Because I had so many issues with the lease, which I described to my client in a very long letter, my client told the tenant that he was unwilling to proceed with the lease on the tenant's form; it would cost too much to negotiate. The tenant agreed, in this instance, to use the landlord's form, but that was not the inevitable outcome. Instead, the deal may simply not have been made.

Even when I have been required, in representing the landlord, to use the tenant's form, I often had to draft an addendum or revision, which basically negated large parts of the tenant's form and substituted the landlord's applicable provisions. In those instances, it appeared to me that the tenant's personnel were required by company policy to have the lease look like the tenant's form, irrespective of what the lease actually said. It was literally a matter

## Documenting the Transaction

of form over substance, which I admit is perplexing to me and not the way I think law (or business) should be practiced.

When it comes to documenting sales contracts, buyers generally prefer to draft the contract—to make the offer, as it were. There is a good reason why buyers want to draft the contract; they are concerned with the condition of the property, the condition of title and with all matters which might haunt them after the closing. Sellers, on the other hand, will generally be walking away with money (unless there is seller financing), and do not want to have any responsibilities after the closing. While the buyer wants all sorts of warranties about the condition of the property, the status of leases, the accuracy of the materials provided by the seller to be used in connection with the buyer's due diligence inspections, the seller would most prefer a contract which states, "Buyer will pay the purchase price and seller will convey the property in "as-is" condition—by quit claim deed."

Still, it is not unusual for seller's counsel to prepare contracts. He or she will use some form which gives the buyer some comfort, but will not usually include the whole alphabet of warranties which the buyer's attorney might insert.

### Forms

Let us assume that you are the person who is to prepare the initial draft of the transaction documents. Where do you start? You will need some sort of form.

There are form books galore. There are forms drafted by bar associations, broker organizations, title companies, banks, trade associations, and legal form companies. There are forms drafted by others in one's firm, which can be found in form files or on the computer.

How good are those forms? As one might expect, the quality of those forms vary widely. Some are old and use language that is archaic, formulaic, or unclear. For example, referring to "the party of the first part" and "the party of the second part" is confusing and silly. Some of these forms are one sided and do not even pretend to be otherwise. Many forms are verbose, inherently ambiguous, unnecessarily long, and contain errors. They may not reflect the law in the jurisdiction where the agreement is being made, or they may still contain provisions that have already been declared unenforceable. Bear in mind that those forms—even those printed in form books or elsewhere—were not written by some supernatural being; they were written by human beings like you and me, people prone to incomplete information and error.

Perhaps we should actually speculate how forms actually came into being. They probably date back to the early days of common law. I have read somewhere that much of the language we now see in documents was first inserted shortly after the Norman invasion of England. Before the invasion, people spoke Anglo-Saxon languages, which are in the Germanic group of languages. The Normans brought in the French, a Latin language. Rather than miss something due to the language differences, many redundancies crept into documents which we, unthinkingly, continue to draft into ours. For example, we "assign, transfer and convey all of seller's right, title and interest" in a property. Does that really differ from we "assign all of seller's interest" in that property? Why do we need eleven words when five will do? It is historical, and these sorts of repetitions really make documents much longer and less readable.[10]

Of course, forms have changed since the year 1066, but not always for the better. For one thing, they have grown longer. There was a certain limitation on the size of documents which had to be written by scribes or clerks, and copied by hand into recorders' books. The typewriter greatly facilitated the expansion of documents, but even that had severe limitations, since typing multiple copies using carbon paper and having to erase errors on all those copies was very time-consuming; revising documents which had been typed was difficult. With the invention of xerography, lawyers were able to revise documents by cutting and pasting. People weaned with the computer may not realize that secretaries literally cut up documents, pasted portions onto paper and photocopied the cut and pasted sheets to create new forms or even signable documents.

---

[10] I highly recommend that all lawyers read HOWARD DARMSTADTER, HEREOF, WHEREOF AND EVERYWHEREOF: A CONTRARIAN GUIDE TO LEGAL DRAFTING (ABA 2002). Darmstadter has studied these issues extensively and writes eloquently (and with great humor) in favor of drafting readable documents.

## Documenting the Transaction

Now that we know how the forms grew, we should ask why they grew. One reason, and perhaps the most justifiable, was to prevent bad things from happening, again. The bad things may have been an adverse court decision which was based on language in the form, but more likely, the bad thing was something that happened to a particular client, who instructed the lawyer to insert something in the form so that "it will never happen to me again."

Another reason documents grow is because of what I call the "lemming effect". A lawyer somewhere thinks of some provision which he or she inserts into his or her lease form. It may be a good provision; or it may make no sense. Another lawyer, negotiating a lease with the first one, sees that provision and decides to add it to his or her form, and so on. The lawyer adding the provision does not really consider whether the provision is a good one or not. The second lawyer merely cuts and pastes the provision into his or her form, sometimes without even reflecting on whether it is consistent with other provisions, or even whether it uses language consistent with the rest of the form. Perhaps that is why we see leases that refer, in one place, to landlord and tenant, and in another place, to lessor and lessee. In one place the premises are referred to as the "Leased Premises" and in other places as the "Demised Premises" or merely the "Premises". Those are dead giveaways. The second lawyer added the provision because he or she assumed that the first lawyer knew something he or she did not know and suspected that the failure to add the provision may somehow subject him or her to criticism or to liability.[11]

That is why it is important to approach forms with a jaundiced eye. Of course, it is difficult to evaluate forms until you have some experience in negotiating deals, and even experienced lawyers sometimes fall into the trap of forms, often using forms on their firm's computer without considering whether they are good forms or not.

---

[11] I wrote an article about one such provision, which I often see in leases. It concerns language that requires tenants to insure their alterations in the premises. If you read the article, I hope you will agree that the provision makes no sense. Sidney Saltz, *Insuring Tenant Improvements*, PROBATE & PROPERTY (Jan.–Feb. 2006), at 45.

*From Handshake to Closing*

When using any form, it is important to remember that the drafter of the form did not know the terms of your transaction. Only you know that! There is no substitute for having the agreement and intent of the parties clearly in mind, and for thorough and thoughtful consideration in the use of forms, or in any drafting, for that matter.

Having said all of that, good forms are still very useful. They cut down the time required to draft documents, they highlight matters to be considered—matters which might otherwise not occur to the drafter, however experienced or skilled, and they create uniformity where that is a consideration. The lawyer in that situation may also have a set of standard inserts or riders to deal with changes frequently negotiated by tenants' counsel. Nevertheless, no matter how familiar the drafter is with the form and the inserts (and even if it is the drafter's own form), it is still essential that those forms be reconsidered with each transaction to assure that the appropriate changes are made to deal with the particular deal and the particular situation, and to incorporate new ideas.

In the leasing situation, it may be wise for the drafter to provide the client with a lease requisition form, which requests the information to be inserted in the lease form, so as to minimize the chance of error, highlight the issues, and minimize the number of communications required.

An experienced lawyer may customarily use his or her own forms, created from other forms but revised over the years to meet problems which have arisen or to reflect that particular lawyer's ideology, or his or her client's way of doing business. Those forms are subject to frequent revision as new issues arise. Less experienced lawyers may not feel confident to do major revisions in other peoples forms and to make them their own. Still, every drafter is obligated to use his or her judgment in using forms, and to make those changes which the drafter feels are warranted under the circumstances and which are necessary to establish the tone which comports with the transaction. Gradually, those revisions will become standard to the drafter and a new form will emerge. That is particularly the case when we can summon up our latest work product on the computer.

## Documenting the Transaction

I have noticed a trend for newer forms to be particularly onerous to the non-drafting party. Much legal time and client expense is required to negotiate an evenhanded deal. While, in the short term, this may appear to be a profitable approach for the drafter, it is not really in the best interest of the client. Even in those situations where the opposing party does not have the economic clout to negotiate the document toward the center, the client is in a transaction with another party that is, legitimately, angry about the manner with which it was dealt.

**The Functions of Drafting**
I should admit to some predilections before proceeding. It is my policy to operate under the assumption that the attorney who is representing the other party to the transaction is an able lawyer. It is a sort of golden rule of drafting (not the lender's golden rule), and it is obviously followed by others as infrequently as the more common golden rule. I knew an attorney who operated on the assumption that his opposing number was a dolt and, as a result, he put provisions in drafts which were at least one-sided, if not totally onerous. He reported that, more often than not, the onerous provisions were not objected to and that he maximized the benefit to his client. Did he really? Did he not actually create a relationship between the parties to the transaction which could become adversarial and hostile? Did his client actually realize on the benefits he inserted in his drafts? Did the negotiation of the document with an able lawyer cost his client much more in fees than it should have?

In any case, now that you have selected your form, you must begin to draft the document. The function of drafting is to memorialize the agreement of the parties. Memorializing agreements between parties to a transaction is one of the most intellectually challenging things a lawyer can perform. There is actually some basis for so many agreements to use the archaism, "Witnesseth" (more about archaisms later). The written agreement witnesses or memorializes an agreement that the parties have already made, either orally or by an exchange of letters or term sheets. This is so whether it is a contract for the purchase and sale of real estate, a lease, documents evidencing and securing a loan, or any other documents. The principal function of the drafter is to see to it that what the parties intend is recorded in the written instruments to be signed by them. This is, of course, not the only function, but it is the one that is, or at least should be, primary. A document that does not meet this requirement will, at best, cost the parties much time and money correcting the error or "blow the deal", or at worst, cause the parties to be involved in litigation to establish their intent, which was not properly documented.

The lawyer drafting the document (or reviewing the other lawyer's draft) has other functions as well. He or she must recognize or anticipate the pitfalls to which his or her client's agreement, as documented, may expose it, and seek to draft the document in such a way as to avoid those pitfalls. Of course, the handshake agreement of the parties may be one which dealt with known problems. For example, the parties may recognize that a property to be purchased has environmental issues which must be resolved as a condition of closing, or a party leasing a building may know that there are impediments to access by people with disabilities which must be removed. More often, however, it is the lawyer for one party or the other who raises those matters, or the possibility of those matters, in his or her draft documents (or objections to the draft). Thus it is the function of the drafter to steer his or her client free from the risks inherent in the agreement which was made and is being documented. That is where the skill of the drafter is most called for.

A third function of the drafter is to seek certain advantages for his or her client. I do not mean to imply that the drafter now has the right to violate my actual golden rule of drafting, but each drafter has a certain license to prefer his or her own client. Certainly, a lawyer drafting a lease for a landlord will use a form which is not totally even-handed; it will be a so-called "landlord lease". Lender forms can be expected to prefer the lender. It is the function of the lawyer presented with these documents for review to recognize that condition and to attempt to negotiate for final documents which favor his own client or which are, at least, more neutral. That lawyer's success will depend on the bargaining power of the respective parties to the transaction.

## Documenting the Transaction

**Drafting for Clarity; Drafting for Readability**

By "drafting for clarity", I am referring to drafting without ambiguity to the extent possible. By "drafting for readability", I am referring to the goal of making the document as comprehensible as possible. It would seem that these goals are compatible, but that is not necessarily so. Nevertheless, both should be the goal of the drafter.[12]

However, I do not advocate the use of so-called "plain English" documents. Many traditional legal phrases are still very useful and, in most cases, are less verbose than the plain English translation. To see what I mean, try rendering "Anything in Section 9 to the contrary notwithstanding" into plain English. The point is that legal language is useful. It is tried and true, in the sense that it has been used for many years and has, in many instances, actually been tested in litigation. Although to many who do not deal in legal documents it might seem to be obtuse jargon, to business people who must read and understand agreements and other documents as part of their daily work, the language becomes as familiar as any other form of writing.

This is not to say that old forms of drafting are necessarily the best. For one thing, I am personally opposed to using archaisms. Terms such as "WITNESSETH", "WHEREAS", "NOW THEREFORE", and "IN WITNESS WHEREOF" relate back to the time when a contract was thought of as a single sentence, with the word, "WITNESSETH" being the verb of that sentence. Obviously that type of drafting contributes nothing but excess verbiage to what is most likely too long an instrument in the first place, and it is best omitted. Nevertheless, it is often appropriate and even helpful that an agreement tell the "story" of the deal. Instead of "WHEREAS" clauses, it may be useful to include a series of Recitals, each preceded by a capital letter. Consideration is still re-

---

[12] Here, again, I refer the reader to Howard Darmstadter's book, *Hereof, Whereof and Everywhereof: A Contrarian Guide to Legal Drafting, supra* note 10. Before reading his book, I emphasized clarity over readability, but have since concluded that they are not inconsistent goals. I recently revised my lease forms to make them more readable. I managed to reduce their length by around 10% without changing the meaning.

*From Handshake to Closing*

quired for a contract, and that should be referred to, even if it is just the mutual undertakings of the parties.

Howard Darmstadter deals extensively with what visual form documents should take. I will not dwell on that, but did you ever notice how difficult it is to read a paragraph that is in all capital letters? It is not you or I. It is actually much more difficult to read because the letters are all the same size. Bold face or underline sufficiently emphasize material, and is much more readable. To show what I mean, compare the following paragraphs in all caps and in bold face.

GRAMMAR. THE MOST VALUABLE TOOL IN DRAFTING, BOTH FOR CLARITY AND READABILITY, IS GOOD GRAMMAR. THE DRAFTER, IF HE OR SHE DOES NOT HAVE A GOOD GROUNDING IN GRAMMAR, SHOULD REALLY BONE UP ON IT, OR READ SOME BOOKS ON STYLE IN WRITING. THIS IS NOT TO SAY THAT THE STYLE OF WRITING RECOMMENDED FOR A NOVEL IS APPROPRIATE FOR LEGAL DRAFTING. FOR EXAMPLE, COMMAS ARE VERY USEFUL IN SEPARATING CONCEPTS AND ENSURING CLARITY, WHEREAS BOOKS ON STYLE MAY NOT ENCOURAGE THE USE OF COMMAS IN THE SAME SITUATIONS. ANOTHER DISPUTE I HAVE WITH STYLISTS IS THE PLACEMENT OF CLOSE QUOTATION MARKS. I THINK THAT IT IS MORE USEFUL, IN MOST SITUATIONS, TO PLACE THE COMMA OR PERIOD OUTSIDE OF THE MARKS, BUT THAT IS ANATHEMA TO GRAMMARIANS. DESPITE THOSE QUIBBLES, AN UNDERSTANDING OF THE ELEMENTS OF STYLE IS MOST HELPFUL.

**Grammar. The most valuable tool in drafting, both for clarity and readability, is good grammar. The drafter, if he or she does not have a good grounding in grammar, should really bone up on it, or read some books on style in writing. This is not to say that the style of writing**

## Documenting the Transaction

recommended for a novel is appropriate for legal drafting. For example, commas are very useful in separating concepts and ensuring clarity, whereas books on style may not encourage the use of commas in the same situations. Another dispute I have with stylists is the placement of close quotation marks. I think that it is more useful, in most situations, to place the comma or period outside of the marks, but that is anathema to grammarians. Despite those quibbles, an understanding of the elements of style is most helpful.

See what I mean?

**Antecedents.** This is closely related to the grammar issue. An antecedent is a word, phrase, or clause to which a pronoun refers. For the purpose of drafting legal documents, I would suggest that it also encompasses a word, phrase, or clause that is qualified or modified by succeeding language, as discussed in the example below. Proper identification of antecedents, even at the cost of repetition, is of critical importance in drafting clear documents. Failure to do so is one of the most common ambiguities, giving rise to much dispute and litigation. A wayward "it" or "they", or the failure to specify which word or series of words or concepts is referred to or qualified by succeeding language, can throw into question material parts of an agreement.

An example of language qualifying a series of concepts ambiguously is as follow: "Landlord shall have the right to enter the Premises with prior oral notice during regular business hours, except in an emergency."[13] Does the phrase, "except in an emergency" modify only the second qualification of Landlord's right, namely the limitation of its right to enter only during business hours, or does it modify the oral notice qualification as well? In this example, the answer is readily apparent because Landlord will not stop to give an oral notice if the Premises are on fire, but the inherent ambiguity in the example can still be recognized. Clearer language would be, "Landlord shall have the right to enter the

---

[13] Here I have placed the quotation marks outside of the period because the period is part of what is being quoted.

Premises with prior oral notice during regular business hours, except that in case of an emergency, Landlord may enter the Premises at any time and without prior notice" It is longer but more clear.

Imprecise reference to antecedents is a ready trap because the drafter "knows" what he or she intends when drafting, and the pronouns are so common. This problem argues for a critical reading and rereading of forms and drafts of documents, with a focus on that issue. The drafter must always consider whether a word, a phrase, or a clause is subject to two or more interpretations.

**Definitions.** Terms that are frequently used in the document should be defined at some point and later used with an initial capital letter. Many documents start out with a whole series of definitions. Although that may be a boon to clarity it certainly does nothing for readability. It is very difficult to focus on a series of definitions when one does not have an understanding of how the defined terms fit into the agreement. It is like reading a list of cities before being presented with the map that locates them. On the other hand, if the drafter waits to define the term until its first use in the document (which is more customary in a brief instrument), it will be difficult for the reader to find that definition when he or she has reached the next use of that term much later in the document. I propose a simple solution for this problem. When a term is defined and followed, as is customary, by a parenthetical such as (the "Owner"), underscored that term so it is easy to spot (the "<u>Owner</u>"). If a glossary is appended to the document and the location of a term's definition (by page or section number) is set out in the glossary, the problem is further eliminated. Certain computer programs enable the drafter or the typist to "mark" the defined terms so that the glossary will be amended automatically if the defined term moves to a different page or is deleted.

**Calculations.** When a calculation is called for in a document, there is an opportunity for ambiguity. I find it useful to describe exactly how it is to be performed. Those old terms, such as quotient, difference, total, fraction, numerator, denominator and the like, which we may have learned in arithmetic, are useful. An example in the

## Documenting the Transaction

document may prove invaluable. Darmstadter advocates using a mathematical formula, instead of trying to describe the calculation in words. My problem is that I find the formula more difficult to use than a verbal description, so I do not do so.[14]

**Brevity.** Polonius says, "Brevity is the soul of wit." Brevity is also the soul of clarity and readability. What we are talking about here is both the length of the document being drafted and the length of its component parts.

Starting with the latter first, the smallest component (other than the word, phrase or clause) is the sentence. While sentences with various clauses and provisos, are an integral part of legal drafting, the drafter should, to the extent consistent with the desired meaning, write in short, expository sentences. An old method of drafting, where every paragraph is a sentence (and the next paragraph starts with the word "And"), may be relatively unambiguous, but it does nothing for the readability of the document (it is, however, consistent with the idea that the entire agreement is a single sentence). When a series of provisions or alternative provisions are included in a sentence, each provision should be preceded by a letter or number, in parentheses, to avoid ambiguity. Similarly, when using the phrase "the lesser of" or "the greater of", it is advisable to use letters or numbers, in parentheses, to separate them, such as in "the lesser of (a) the cost of remediation and (b) the sum of $100,000" (by the way, "and" is the correct conjunction).[15]

The next component is the Section or Paragraph. In this regard, it is helpful if the document follows a sort of outline form, with groups of Sections pertaining to a subject matter being in the largest group (often called an Article), followed by Sections, Subsections, and so on. For ease of reference in other portions of the agreement (or in later amendments of the document), a number or

---

[14] Notice the use of the word "verbal", which means, "in words". A common error is the use of the word "verbal" when "oral" or "spoken" is meant.

[15] Darmstadter also advises against the use of both words and numerals when referring to amounts. It is fatal to readability and creates the possibility of inconsistency. It is not necessarily true that the words govern. *See* Prudential Ins. Co. of America v. SS American Lancer, 870 F.2d 867 (2d Cir. 1989).

letter should precede each section and subsection. That avoids the necessity of referring to provisions as, for example, "the third grammatical paragraph of Section 3".[16]

How long should the instrument be? The answer appears simple. It should be long enough to document the agreement of the parties. It must also protect the drafter's client from possible adverse consequences. Aye, there's the rub. In my opinion, most documents are too long (and they are growing). They contain provisions that are onerous, redundant, unnecessary, and inappropriate.

I have already discussed my "golden rule of drafting" in connection with onerous provisions. Nevertheless, many documents contain them, or at least provisions which are "throwaway clauses"—provisions that are included for the purpose of having something to negotiate out of the document. Throwaway clauses may be useful in a situation where the parties have relatively equal bargaining power. If the drafter tenders a document that is perfectly even-handed, not only may he or she shock the opposing attorney, but that attorney will have no ammunition, nothing to discuss. A limited number of such clauses are not objectionable, provided they are not too obvious or too onerous. If they are not negotiated out of the document, they may give the drafter's client some advantage without hurting the other side too badly. If, on the other hand, the drafter's client has a substantial economic advantage, such as a landlord in a shopping center which is negotiating a lease with a small tenant, throwaway clauses will simply bully his or her counterpart, and violate the "golden rule of drafting". (Bear in mind that one party's throwaway clause may be another's deal point, so just because it looks, feels, and tastes like a throwaway clause, it may not be to your counterpart.)[17]

Redundancy also presents a problem, and often an unintended one. As I pointed out, documents often are drafted by incorporating applicable provisions from various prior documents. This may sometimes be a useful technique, but it can be a danger-

---

[16] I prefer "Section" to "Paragraph", but that is a personal preference.

[17] I use the word "counterpart" rather than "opponent" on the assumption that the other attorney in the deal is interested in concluding a reasonable deal; I may be giving that lawyer the benefit of the doubt, but let us assume good faith.

## Documenting the Transaction

ous one. Aside from the obvious need to conform defined terminology (as in making certain that "Landlord" is referred to as such, and not occasionally as "Lessor"), it is important to be certain that concepts that are repeated are totally consistent. Inconsistency is a fertile ground for litigation. It may be better simply to cross-reference.

Documents often contain provisions which are unnecessary, and they lengthen the document inordinately. My favorite example is the provision which permits documents to be signed in counterparts.[18] The Statute of Frauds requires only that a document be signed by "the party to be charged". It does not require that they physically sign the same copy of the document. Notwithstanding that, one sometimes sees counterpart language that is several sentences long.

Likewise, drafters often include language that is inappropriate. I feel that a layperson's warranty of the enforceability of a document should never be included. For one thing, it constitutes a legal conclusion, not a factual statement. Secondly, it does not usually contain the numerous qualifications that lawyers customarily include in enforceability opinions, rendering the warranty far too broad. Another provision that is used too indiscriminately is the default phrase "or an event which may, with notice or expiration of time, or both, become an event of default." That phrase (which is ambiguous to start with), is often used in many situations to which it does not really apply. Even more serious is the piling on of warranties, some of which are not only inappropriate, but onerous as well. I will discuss warranties further below.

How do documents get too long? As I said before, lawyers are notorious copycats. When we see language in another lawyer's draft, we often incorporate it into our forms and our documents. In many cases, that is advisable, because new language frequently results from the rethinking of old ideas, reaction to court rulings or simply a decision that a bad thing which happened to one's client will never happen again. On the other hand, the new language to be

---

[18] Darmstadter gives a history of the concept—it arose when one copy of an agreement was drafted, and it was torn apart so each party had a counterpart. The entire agreement could be proved by matching the parts. DARMSTADTER, *supra* note 10, at 104–105.

incorporated may be onerous, redundant, unnecessary, or inappropriate, being the faults described above. Just as one should not assume that one's opponent is a dolt, one should not assume that the creator of new language is omniscient. There is no substitute for the drafter's own careful analysis and consideration.

**The Case of the Proliferating Adjectives**
Have you ever seen the phrase, "sole, absolute, and unfettered discretion"? Or better, "for any reason or no reason at Landlord's sole, absolute and unfettered discretion"? Why did the drafter need any 13, or even five, words to make the case for a party's discretion when one word will do? In my opinion the word "discretion" means, well, discretion, not "reasonable judgment". That makes the phrase "reasonable discretion" an oxymoron. However, I have been met with an argument from lawyers I respect to the effect that judges may look for some basis to require a party to be reasonable where he or she did not intend that requirement, and for that reason, at least the adjective "sole" should be added.

It is true that judges are unpredictable and may look for some basis on which to base their decisions as they seek to be "just" as well as within the law. I recently was confronted with this argument and, although rather stubbornly I refused to add the word "sole" each time the word "discretion" appeared, I did agree to add a definition of "discretion" at the end of the document. I was tempted to say that "Discretion means discretion", but instead I came up with the following: "The use of the term 'discretion' shall not imply an obligation on the person having discretion to act reasonably, but the word shall be construed based on its true definition." My counterpart was satisfied.

**Dispute Resolution**
Trying to second-guess what a judge may decide is often what drafting is about. Although we draft and negotiate documents to clearly set out the parties' rights and obligations, we must always be mindful that a dispute may arise between them. If that occurs, it is hoped that the parties and their counsel will seek to amicably resolve their differences by agreeing on what was intended or by renegotiating the agreement in some mutually acceptable manner.

## Documenting the Transaction

If that is not successful, the parties may avail themselves of some of the various alternative dispute resolution techniques, such as mediation. The ultimate recourse, however, is to litigation, or if the parties have so provided or otherwise agree, to arbitration. Whether the parties litigate or arbitrate, they become involved in an adversarial forum, where the decision as to the meaning of the document and the rights and obligations of the parties are, in the absence of settlement along the way, determined by a disinterested third party.

While arbitrators may (or may not) be experts in real estate, most judges will have spent their careers before becoming judges doing litigation—often criminal litigation. They may or may not have experience with real estate transactions or even the separate body of real estate law, and may not have a keen sense as to the nuances which we carefully crafted into our documents. They may even have some sense of the "justice" of the given situation which is totally at odds with the intention of the parties or the careful compromises reached at the negotiating table, or what is customary in real estate transactions. That is why it is particularly important to draft clearly and carefully. All documents should end up having been drafted with the assumption that the person ultimately determining what they mean will have little or no sophistication in real estate matters.

**Vagueness**
It is commonly perceived that former Secretary of State Henry Kissinger, when negotiating deals with other countries, would try to get agreement on certain contentious issues by incorporating vagueness or ambiguity into the document under discussion. That way, if the problem under discussion does not occur, the balance of the agreement can still be implemented. If the problem does occur, then there would, it was hoped, be an opportunity for further diplomacy. Certainly it is possible to draft and negotiate real estate documents in the same way, but unfortunately, there may never be an occasion for future diplomacy. Yes, if a problem comes up after the document has been signed and the provision in question is vague or ambiguous, the parties usually have some chance to resolve the matter on their own. If they fail to do so, there is fortu-

nately (or unfortunately), an alternative. Unlike the result of the ultimate failure of diplomacy, which is armed conflict, the alternative is litigation. However, litigation is, as I have shown, not very attractive either. Thus it is very important, when drafting documents, to try to avoid vagueness or ambiguity. The only thing worse than having your client in litigation defending the language that you drafted, is to have him or her in that litigation, and losing the case.

Another way vagueness may arise is through the use of long, convoluted sentences. If you have to read the sentence more than twice to get its meaning, and still have problems understanding it, think how a judge will feel. Just for fun, try reading the following sentence regarding a letter of credit. I actually had to review it in a recent lease negotiation (I am aware that you do not know the nature of the deal agreed to, but just try to figure it out; imagine you are the judge):

> **If the required amount of the Letter of Credit is not reduced due to a Base Rent payment or on a date specified above because of the existence of an Event of Default and/or because Tenant is a debtor subject to a bankruptcy proceeding, the reduction shall occur when and if the Event of Default is cured and/or Tenant ceases to be a debtor subject to a bankruptcy proceeding, as applicable, and Landlord shall promptly notify Tenant and the issuer of the Letter of Credit, in writing, of such cure or cessation, as applicable, and shall further promptly provide to the issuer of the Letter of Credit such revocations of any "No Reduction Notice" (as defined in the Letter of Credit) and/or other documents as such issuer or Tenant may request ("LC Reduction Consent Documents") in order to consent to the reduction of the Letter of Credit, and to cause the Letter of Credit to be reduced, to the amount required by this Lease and that would have been applicable under the Letter of Credit if Landlord had not**

delivered any such No Reduction Notice(s) to such issuer (and, in such regard, if Landlord delivers a No Reduction Notice as aforesaid because Tenant is a debtor subject to a bankruptcy proceeding and before the required amount of the Letter of Credit has been reduced to $1,000,000.00, Landlord further agrees to promptly delivery to the issuer of the Letter of Credit LC Reduction Consent Documents that consent to reductions of the Letter of Credit, and cause the Letter of Credit to be reduced, on account of any Base Rent payments received by Landlord (whether directly from Tenant or pursuant to a draw(s) on the Letter of Credit) that, but, for the delivery of such No Reduction Notice, would have resulted in a reduction of the Letter of Credit under subsection (a) above).

Need I say more about long, convoluted sentences?

There is a handy rule of construction that courts use to decide cases where the provision in question is vague or ambiguous and the court cannot figure out what was intended by the parties. That rule states that the provision is to be construed most strongly against the party drafting the document. While the rule may seem harsh and, as we shall see, drafters sometimes seek to negate it, it is actually a very useful tool for deciding cases. Assume you are the judge confronting such a provision. One side argues that it means A and the other that it means B. Neither side is convincing because the language is too vague or ambiguous to determine on its face what was intended. In that situation, parol evidence may be admissible to determine the intent of the parties, but that evidence may not be convincing; in fact, the parties might never really have considered or discussed the language under discussion. Still, the judge must decide the case because that is his or her job. Here the rule of construction comes into play. Of course it punishes the party whose lawyer drafted the language, and it embarrasses the lawyer, but who else should suffer? Is it fair that the other party should lose?

*From Handshake to Closing*

Many documents now expressly provide that the rule of construction should not be applied. They recite that there was extensive negotiation of the document and that, in effect, both parties drafted the document and therefore the rule cannot be applied. I really do not know how judges react to that provision, but if I were a judge, I would ignore it. Even if there actually were extensive negotiation, one party or the other drafted the provision in question. In fact, the vague or ambiguous provision may not have been the subject of negotiation at all, so how can it be said that both parties drafted it. The judge hearing the matter must still decide the case, and he or she has no real help from the parties. The easiest course is to either ignore the provision regarding joint drafting or to hold that the provision embodies a fiction which the judge is not only free to disregard, but is obligated to do so.

Let us examine a common vague provision in the fire and casualty section of a lease. That provision states that if there is a fire or other casualty that renders the premises untenantable, the landlord may terminate the lease. Assume that the tenant occupies the $20^{th}$ floor of a 30-story building and that there is a fire on the $25^{th}$ floor, that there is no fire damage in the $20^{th}$ floor premises, but the water used to put the fire out has seeped into the $20^{th}$ floor tenant's space. The water must be drained, the walls repaired or at least repainted, the carpeting replaced, and other work done, all of which will take about a month. The tenant cannot occupy the premises while the work is being done. Instead, assume that there was no damage to the 20th-floor tenant at all, but the elevators are put out of order for two weeks, or the fire department is insisting that no one occupy the building until it is inspected fully and determined to be safe. In each of those situations, the 20th-floor tenant's space is untenantable. What if this tenant happens to have a very favorable rental rate and the landlord can lease the space for a lot more money? What landlord would not leap at the opportunity to terminate the lease under those circumstances? But was this what was really intended by the parties? By using the word "untenantable" the drafter, as well as the other lawyer probably contemplated major damage to the premises. They could easily have provided a time period of untenantability, such a six months, or they could have tied the right to terminate to a loss which cost over a certain sum to repair (or a percentage of the total replacement cost of the premises), but in my example, they did not do so. They left the provision vague.

It is doubtful that this provision was even discussed by the parties or their counsel during the negotiations. If it had been, the language would probably have been tightened up. But a fire or other casualty is not a common occurrence, so why spend a lot of time and run up the fees to talk about it? The problem is that while fires are not common, they do occur. Our tenant does not want to lose its favorable lease, so it is prepared to litigate. Hence the application of the rule of construction.

I do not include a provision seeking to negate the rule in my documents. I feel it is my responsibility to consider all the possible issues and to avoid vagueness or ambiguity. Do I always succeed? Of course not. But it is still my job and I am prepared to accept the consequences. I have found that lawyers who do include such a provision are very loathe to remove it, but I do not fight too hard on this point. I have enough confidence in the judiciary that the provision will not withstand scrutiny, or that the judge will find an equitable way around it.

**Some Substantive Provisions**

It is not the intention of this work to set forth a host of substantive provisions. I will leave that to the writers of treatises or of formbooks. On the other hand, I believe it is useful to discuss some substantive provisions that I insert in leases or contracts, both to give a flavor of my drafting and to provide some material for consideration when I discuss, in the next chapter, the analysis of documents prepared by others.

The first provision I will discuss is a lease section I developed dealing with the allocation of insurable risks. The section reads, at length, as follows:

*From Handshake to Closing*

## I. RISK ALLOCATION AND INSURANCE

1. **Allocation of Risks.** The parties desire, to the extent permitted by law, to allocate certain risks of personal injury, bodily injury or property damage, and risks of loss of real or personal property by reason of fire, explosion or other casualty, and to provide for the responsibility for insuring those risks. It is the intent of the parties that, to the extent any event is insured for or required in this Lease to be insured for, any loss, cost, damage, or expense arising from such event, including the expense of defense against claims or suits, be paid out of insurance proceeds, without regard to the fault of Tenant, its officers, employees or agents (the "Tenant Protected Parties"), and without regard to the fault of Landlord, its beneficiary (if Landlord is a land trust), Agent, their respective partners, shareholders, members, agents, directors, officers and employees (the "Landlord Protected Parties"). As between the Landlord Protected Parties and the Tenant Protected Parties, those risks are allocated as follows:

    (a) Tenant shall bear the risk of bodily injury, personal injury or death, or damage to property, of third persons occasioned by events occurring on or about the Leased Premises, regardless of the party at fault. Those risks shall be insured as provided in Section 2(a).

    (b) Landlord shall bear the risk of bodily injury, personal injury, or death or damage to the property of third persons occasioned by events occurring on or about the Real Estate (other than premises leased to tenants), provided that event is occasioned by the wrongful act or omission of any of Landlord Protected Parties. That risk shall be insured against as provided in Section 3(a).

    (c) Tenant shall bear the risk of damage to Tenant's contents, trade fixtures, machinery, equipment, furniture, and furnishings ("Personalty") in the Leased Premises arising out of loss by the events required to be insured against pursuant to Section 2(b).

## Documenting the Transaction

(d) Landlord shall bear the risk of damage to the building on the Real Estate arising out of loss by events required to be insured against pursuant to Section 3(b).

Notwithstanding the foregoing, provided the party required to carry insurance under Section 2(a) or Section 3(a) does not default in its obligation to do so, if and to the extent that any loss occasioned by any event of the type described in Section 1(a) or Section 1(b) exceeds the coverage or the amount of insurance required to be carried under those Sections or such greater coverage or amount of insurance as is actually carried, or results from an event not required to be insured against or not actually insured against, the party at fault shall pay the amount not actually covered.

2. **Tenant's Insurance.** Tenant shall procure and maintain policies of insurance, at its cost insuring:

(a) The Landlord Protected Parties (as "named insureds"), and Landlord's mortgagee, if any, of which Tenant is given notice, and the Tenant Protected Parties, from all claims, demands or actions made by or on behalf of any person, persons or entity and arising from, related to or connected with the Leased Premises, for bodily injury to or personal injury to or death of any person, or more than one person, or for damage to property, in an amount of not less than $3 million combined single limit per occurrence/aggregate. That insurance shall be written on an "occurrence" basis and not on a "claims made" basis. If at any time during the Term, Tenant owns or rents more than one location, the policy shall contain an endorsement to the effect that the aggregate limit in the policy shall apply separately to each location owned or rented by Tenant. Landlord shall have the right, exercisable by giving notice to Tenant, to require Tenant to increase that limit if, in Landlord's reasonable judgment, that amount is insufficient to protect the Landlord Protected Parties and the Tenant Protected Parties from judgments which might result from those claims, demands, or actions. If Tenant is unable, despite reasonable efforts in good faith, to cause its liability insurer to insure the Landlord Protected Parties as "named insureds", Tenant shall nevertheless cause the Landlord Protected Parties to be insured as "additional insureds", and Tenant will protect, indemnify and save harmless the Landlord Protected Parties from and against any and all liabilities, obligations, claims, damages, penalties, causes of action, costs, and expenses (including reasonable attorney's fees and expenses) imposed upon or incurred by or asserted against the Landlord Protected Parties, or any of them, by reason of any bodily injury to or personal injury to or death of any person or more than one person or for damage to property, occurring on or about the Leased Premises, caused by any party including any Landlord Protected Party, to the extent of the amount of the insurance required to be carried under this Section 6.1(a) or such greater amount of insurance as Tenant actually carries. Tenant shall cause its liability insurance to include contractual liability coverage fully covering this indemnity.

(b) All contents and Tenant's trade fixtures, machinery, equipment, furniture, and furnishings in the Leased Premises to the extent of at least 90% of their replacement cost under Standard Fire and Extended Coverage Policy and all other risks of direct physical loss as insured against under Special Form ("all risk" coverage). The insurance shall contain an endorsement waiving the insurer's right of subrogation against any Landlord Protected Party, provided that the waiver of the right of subrogation shall not be operative in any case where its effect is to invalidate the insurance coverage or increase its cost. In case of increased cost, Tenant shall promptly give Landlord notice and Landlord shall have the right, within 30 days after that notice, to pay any increased cost, and keep the waiver in full force and effect.

(c) Tenant Protected Parties from all worker's compensation claims.

(d) Landlord and Tenant against breakage of all plate glass utilized in the improvements on the Leased Premises.

## Documenting the Transaction

3. **Landlord's Insurance.** Landlord shall procure and maintain policies of insurance insuring:

    (a) All claims, demands, or actions made by or on behalf of any person, persons or entity and arising from, related to or connected with the Real Estate (other than premises leased to tenants), for bodily injury to or personal injury to or death of any person, or more than 1 person, or for damage to property in an amount of not less than $3 million combined single limit per occurrence/aggregate. That insurance shall be written on an "occurrence" basis and not on a "claims made" basis. If at any time during the Term, Landlord owns more than one location, the policy shall contain an endorsement to the effect that the aggregate limit in the policy shall apply separately to each location owned by Landlord.

    (b) The improvements at any time situated upon the Real Estate against loss or damage by fire, lightning, wind storm, hail storm, aircraft, vehicles, smoke, explosion, riot or civil commotion as provided by the Standard Fire and Extended Coverage Policy and all other risks of direct physical loss as insured against under Special Form ("all risk" coverage). The insurance coverage shall be for not less than 90% of the full replacement cost of such improvements with agreed amount endorsement. Landlord shall be named as the insured and all proceeds of insurance shall be payable to Landlord. The insurance shall contain an endorsement waiving the insurer's right of subrogation against any Tenant Protected Party, provided that the waiver of the right of subrogation shall not be operative in any case where the effect thereof is to invalidate such insurance coverage or increase its cost. In case of increased cost, Landlord shall promptly give Tenant notice thereof and Tenant shall have the right, within 30 days after that notice, to pay any increased cost, and keep the waiver in full force and effect.

*From Handshake to Closing*

    (c) Landlord's business income, protecting Landlord from loss of rents and other charges during the period while the Leased Premises are untenantable due to fire or other casualty (for the period reasonably determined by Landlord).

    (d) Flood or earthquake insurance whenever, in Landlord's reasonable judgment, that protection is necessary and it is available at commercially reasonable cost.

4. **Form of Insurance. All of the insurance shall be in responsible companies. As to Tenant's insurance, the insurer and the form, substance and amount (where not stated above) shall be satisfactory from time to time to Landlord and any mortgagee of Landlord, and shall unconditionally provide that it is not subject to cancellation or non-renewal except after at least 30 days' prior notice to Landlord and any mortgagee of Landlord. Originals of Tenant's insurance policies (or certificates satisfactory to Landlord), together with satisfactory evidence of payment of the premiums, shall be delivered to Agent at the Commencement Date, and renewals not less than 30 days prior to the end of the term of the coverage.**

    Even a cursory reading will show that the above language is different from insurance provisions encountered in most leases.[19] That is because its purpose is not the usual one, which is to impose liability for all insurable risks on tenants, but to eliminate risk based on fault to the extent that the risk referred to is insurable under insurance obtainable by the parties at commercially reasonable rates. It requires the landlord to carry property insurance on the building, as it exists (including, necessarily, insurance on the leasehold improvements and on alterations performed by tenants), and also incorporates full waivers of claims and the rights of subrogation. The language is intended to be even-handed and, although I sometimes encounter resistance from tenants who want

---

[19] I will present an example of a more customary form below when I discuss analyzing other drafter's documents.

to limit liability to situations where they are at fault, an explanation of the purpose of the provision, plus the tenants' ascertaining that their liability insurance covers the risks, usually solves the problem.[20]

The other provision I will discuss is the warranties language I typically insert in real estate sales contracts, where I represent the purchaser:

1. **Condition Warranties. Seller represents and warrants to Purchaser regarding the condition of the Property as follows:**
   (a) The roof and foundation are in good condition, free from leaks and seepage.

   (b) The heating equipment and the air conditioning equipment are in good operating condition and repair.

   (c) The plumbing and electrical systems are in good operating condition and repair.

   (d) The building on the Property is in sound structural condition, and contains no asbestos.

   (e) Seller has not used, treated, stored, or disposed of any Hazardous Substances (as hereinafter defined) on, about or under the Real Estate. Seller shall have and retain, and shall release, defend, hold harmless and indemnify Purchaser, its directors, officers and assignees from and against, any Environmental Liabilities related to Environmental Conditions on, about or under the Real Estate to the extent that the Liabilities arise from acts and conditions existing on or taking place prior to the Closing or which relate to Seller's actions, inactions or operations prior to Closing; provided however, if after the Closing, actions or inactions of Purchaser contribute to any material extent to the Environmental

---

[20] For a full discussion of this issue, see my article, *Allocation of Insurable Risks in Commercial Leases*, 37 REAL PROPERTY PROBATE J. 479 (Fall 2002).

Conditions giving rise to Environmental Liabilities, then to the extent Seller is damaged by such actions or inactions, Purchaser shall have and assume, and shall release, defend, hold harmless and indemnify Seller from and against, all such Environmental Liabilities.

(i) "Environmental Conditions" means and refers to all conditions relating to Hazardous Substances present on, under or emanating from the Real Estate (including, but not limited to the use, storage, disposal, emission, release or discharge of any such substance.)

(ii) "Environmental Liabilities" includes, without limitation, any cost, expense, loss, liability, obligation, damage (including but not limited to any fine, civil penalty, judgment or award) payable or due any person, entity or government agency, including any sums paid in settlement for any such liabilities together with reasonable attorneys fees and other expenses incurred in investigating, commencing, defending or settling any litigation or other proceeding, commenced, threatened, or incidental to any of the foregoing, arising from any Environmental Condition.

(iii) "Environmental Law" includes and refers to any Federal, State or local law, statute, ordinance, rule, regulation or code now or hereafter promulgated relating to the protection, preservation or restoration of the environment (including, without limitation, air, water vapor, surface water, groundwater, drinking water supply, surface land, subsurface land, plant and animal life, or any other natural resource), or to human health or safety, or the exposure to, or the use, storage, recycling, treatment, generation, transportation, proceeding, handling, labeling, production, release or disposal of Hazardous Substances.

## Documenting the Transaction

    (iv)     "Hazardous Substances" means any substance deemed or classified as hazardous, dangerous, toxic, radioactive, or otherwise regulated under any Environmental Law. Hazardous Substance shall include, without limitation, petroleum products and by-products and asbestos.

(f) The Real Estate is not located in a flood plain or special flood hazard zone.

(g) No portion of the Real Estate is a "wetlands", as defined in the federal Clean Water Act, and no dredge and fill permit or similar authorization is required in order to develop the Real Estate.

(h) There are no underground storage tanks on the Real Estate and, to the best knowledge of Seller, there have not been underground storage tanks on the Real Estate at any prior time.

(i) The Property complies with applicable requirements of the Americans with Disabilities Act, and with state and local laws, ordinances, and regulations pertaining to access by persons with disabilities.

2. **Lease Warranties.** Seller represents and warrants to Purchaser and covenants with respect to the leases affecting the Property.

    (a) The only leases affecting the Property are those certain leases described on <u>Exhibit A</u> attached hereto (the "Leases"). Within 5 days after the date hereof, Seller shall deliver to Purchaser a true and correct copy of the Leases and all amendments or modifications thereto. Seller shall not execute or consent to any further leases, or amendments or modifications to the Leases prior to Closing without Purchaser's prior written consent.

    (b) No tenants (the "Tenants") are in default under the Leases. Seller, as landlord, is not in default under any of the Leases. None of the Tenants have prepaid rent for more than the current month.

(c) The Tenants are in possession of the respective premises demised to them under the Leases.

(d) None of the Tenants have made any claim of default by Seller under the Leases. Seller shall promptly deliver to Purchaser copies of any notices hereafter received by Seller from any Tenant relating to the Leases. None of the Tenants has contested the manner by which its allocable share of real estate taxes, operating expenses, or common area maintenance expenses are calculated or any other matter under its Lease, nor has any Tenant exercised any right (or claimed right) of retention or set-off whatsoever against the rents payable under its Lease.

(e) Any and all work to be performed by the landlord under the Leases has been completed and paid for.

(f) There are no outstanding and unpaid leasing commissions due to any broker and no leasing commissions which may accrue to any broker under any agreement relating to the extension of any lease term or the exercise of any option relative to the Property.

(g) There are no unexpired rent concessions under the Leases, and there are no rights or options to extend, to lease additional space or to terminate the Lease, and no purchase options under the Leases, except as disclosed in **Exhibit A**.

(h) The security deposits ("Security Deposits") under the Leases, in the aggregate, equal $_____, as set forth individually on the Schedule of Leases attached hereto as **Exhibit A**, none of which have been applied by Seller to cure any default of any Tenant. Seller shall grant to Purchaser at Closing a credit against the Pur-

## Documenting the Transaction

chase Price in the full amount of the Security Deposits, including accrued interest thereon (if any), and shall assign and deliver to Purchaser any passbooks, letters of credit, certificates of deposit or any other instruments evidencing or relating to the Security Deposits or delivered to the landlord under the Leases in lieu of a Security Deposit.

(i) Seller has no business relationship with any of the Tenants except as landlord and tenant.

3. **Further Warranties and Covenants.** Seller further represents, warrants to and covenants with Purchaser as follows:

   (a) Seller owns fee simple title to the Property, free and clear of all encumbrances.

   (b) All financial data delivered to Purchaser hereunder are true, correct and complete and all copies of books and records are true, correct and complete copies of same.

   (c) There are no service contracts or equipment leases relating to the Property to which Seller is a party ("Service Contracts"), except as set forth in <u>Exhibit B</u> attached hereto and made a part hereof. Seller shall deliver to Purchaser, within 20 days after the execution and delivery hereof, copies of all Service Contracts, and shall assign to Purchaser at Closing (to the extent assignable) such of the Service Contracts as Purchaser shall determine.

   (d) Seller has no employees with respect to the operation and maintenance of Property.

   (e) There exists no management agreement or exclusive brokerage agreement that will continue in force beyond the Closing date.

   (f) The improvements on the Property have been constructed pursuant to building permits validly issued by

*From Handshake to Closing*

the municipality of _____, and substantially in accordance with the plans and specifications delivered to Purchaser, and a certificate of occupancy has been issued in connection with the completed structure. Seller has not received any notice of, and has no knowledge of any violations (not heretofore corrected) of any applicable laws or ordinances relative to the Property or the business now being conducted thereon. Seller agrees to correct any violation of which it receives notice prior to Closing.

(g) There is no pending or, to Seller's knowledge, threatened (1) condemnation of any part of the Real Estate by any governmental authority; (2) special assessment against the Real Estate; (3) increased assessment for real estate taxes over the assessment used with respect to most recent year for which the real estate taxes were payable; or (4) action against Seller for breach of any restrictive covenant affecting the Real Estate.

(h) Access to the Real Estate is by open, dedicated public streets.

(i) Seller shall maintain, or shall cause to be maintained, the Property in the same condition as of the date hereof until Closing, reasonable wear and tear or loss by fire or other casualty excepted.

(j) The Real Estate is zoned _____, which zoning classification allows Seller or the present occupants to conduct their businesses, as is now being conducted, as a permitted use.

(k) Seller has not used or intended to use the Property in any manner, to commit, or facilitate the commission of violation of the Federal Comprehensive Drug Abuse Prevention and Control Act of 1970, as amended, and Seller has not subjected the Property or any part thereof to forfeiture under the Illinois Controlled Sub-

## Documenting the Transaction

stances Act, the Cannabis Control Act, or any similar statute.

(l) Seller is not a "foreign person" within the meaning of Section 1445 of the Internal Revenue Code.

The above warranties are not, I feel, unreasonable for a purchaser to request. Whether they are consistent with the deal or are reasonable for a seller to agree to is another matter, and one I shall deal with when I discuss the review and negotiation of documents, below.

**Boilerplate**
Boilerplate can be defined as provisions which appear in most documents, but which do not mean very much.

It is my firm conviction that there is no such thing as "boilerplate" because every provision in a document has economic impact. Take the warranty of enforceability described above. It was inserted for some purpose, albeit a poor one (in my judgment). If the party who made that warranty—without thinking because it was "boilerplate"—is sued because some provision in the document is not enforceable, that party may be sorry he or she did not consider it more fully.

Take the notice clause, as another example. Who even reads those? Many notice clauses provide for the giving of notice by registered or certified mail, and the notice is effective three days after mailing. Have you mailed something by certified mail lately? Try mailing a "notice" to yourself by that method. I will wager that it will not arrive in three days; it may not arrive in one week. What happened to your grace period to cure? It has been eaten up in the United States Postal Service. It is my view that notices that require or permit a responsive action (such as curing a default) should be effective on receipt or refusal. Other notices (such as exercising a option or a right to terminate) may be effective when sent.

These are simply examples of the importance of drafting every provision of the document as one which is there for a purpose; its purpose is to affect the rights and obligations of the parties, because that is exactly what it does.

## A Final Word

No matter how long you have worked on drafting a document, no matter how many times you have used the same form or the inserts, it is of critical importance that you re-read the document before it goes to your client or its broker, and certainly to your counterpart. In fact, the longer you have worked on that document, the more you need to re-read it. It is amazing how many errors, redundancies, omissions, inconsistencies or even typos slip into documents. Does it not sometimes seem that there are demons that hover over your computer and change your otherwise perfect draft? I even found them inserting unwelcome matters into this book. Re-reading may be tedious and time-consuming, and you may not even be able to charge for the time, but it may save you considerable embarrassment, or worse.

## Conclusion

Drafting is not easy. It requires careful and thoughtful consideration. Forms are helpful, but must not be used uncritically. Time and effort are essential. Still, the drafting of clear and readable instruments that appropriately meet the needs of the drafter's client and properly document the agreement of the parties is one of the most intellectually challenging and rewarding aspects of the transactional lawyer's career.

## Reviewing and Analyzing Documents

I always find that reviewing and analyzing documents is much more difficult than drafting. Except for the novice drafter or someone using a form for the first time, the lawyer drafting documents tends to be aware of the contents or at least, the thrust, of the form. Most forms tend to be one-sided, in favor of the party on whose behalf the document is being drafted, so if there is a bias or error, it is in favor of the drafter's client. Thus, when reviewing someone else's draft, it is incumbent on the reviewing lawyer to find those biases, evaluate their impact and, at least, call them to the client's attention.

The most important thing for the reviewing lawyer to keep in mind is his or her understanding of what the deal is. The most even-handed paperwork will not do if it erroneously documents the agreement that the parties have reached. In this regard, I am referring not only to the broad outline of the deal, such as purchase price or rent, but such important ancillary matters as whether a sale is "as is" or the extent the rent is net or gross.[21]

Another important thing a reviewing lawyer must do is consider the client's bargaining position. This does not mean that if the client has little leverage, the review can be cursory—quite the contrary. The client may not be able to accomplish much in negotiations, but it certainly ought to understand the risks of the transaction. A client renting 1,100 square feet of office area may not

---

[21] In a "net" lease, all of the taxes and other expenses of landlord in connection with the property are passed through to the tenant; if the tenant is leasing only a part of the property, the tenant pays its pro rata share of those expenses. While that is the general definition of "net", it is not always used that way: the landlord may assume the obligation to pay for repairs or replacements of the roof and structure, for example, with the tenant paying the remaining expenses. In a "gross" lease, the landlord pays those expenses (although they are factored into the base rent). In a "modified gross" lease, those expenses are included in the base rent, but the tenant pays the excess over a base amount.

want to spend a lot of money for a thorough review, but it is the lawyer's professional responsibility to give as full a review of that lease as any other, and if the client does not want to pay for that, it is better for the lawyer to withdraw than to skim through the lease and have to answer later for having missed something important. Negotiating that 1,100 square foot lease may be another matter, but more on that later.

Reviewing someone else's draft document is difficult. There are various reasons for this. Other drafters may not be as concerned about readability as you now are. The document may be long, perhaps overlong, redundant, inconsistent, and totally one sided. Remember, you are not merely reading the document; you are trying to find provisions which are not consistent with the agreement of the parties or which constitute overreaching. You cannot speed-read the document, as you might a novel or a magazine article; you cannot even read it as you would read non-fiction. The document must be read closely, and you should never assume that the document will say what you think it will. If time permits, and the document is complicated, it may be wise to reread the document.

I had an experience which illustrates this. I was reviewing a lease and, in reading the assignment and subletting section, I encountered a provision dealing with the landlord's right to exclude, from the premises, space that the tenant proposes to sublease. That is commonly known as a "recapture right" and it is not an uncommon provision and generally it is not a particularly objectionable one. The lease went on to state that the rent would be adjusted after the space was excluded. The basis for the rent adjustment was something the reviewer might make an assumption about—that the rent would be reduced pro rata. This lease did say that, but included language which provided that the adjusted rent would be *based on the rent per square foot then being quoted by the landlord for other space in the building.* In other words, if the tenant proposed to sublease less than the entire premises, the rent payable after the exclusion could very well be greater than the rent for the entire premises before the proposed sublease was negotiated. The offending language was deliberately written in a sort of offhand manner so as to be easily missed. I feel that if I had missed that, I

## Reviewing and Analyzing Documents

might well have been committing malpractice, particularly since the provision was so onerous and the result could have been so damaging. The landlord's attorney agreed to delete the provision without even making an argument but, needless to say, I went back over the entire lease very carefully to make certain that there were no other zingers in it.

When I review a document, I generally make marginal notes as I go along. Although I am pretty careful to make my notes legible, I doubt that they would really be intelligible to others. I write "no" or "X" or put question marks, or I write "cl", which means that there is an issue requiring the client's decision. Sometimes I will write "silly" if I think some provision is not unacceptable, but makes little sense. My method is really uniquely my own, and when another reviewer examines a document, he or she will have a totally different method of noting issues. Some lawyers will make comments on a yellow pad; others may use many different colored pens or pencils. It does not matter what method you use, so long as you can interpret your notations, and so long as you highlight the issues you plan to raise with your client or with your counterpart.

**Examples**

Again, it is not my intention to go through an entire contract or lease to show what I would or would not object to. However, some examples may be useful.

First, take those warranties I had so carefully drafted, and which are set out on page 43.

What is wrong with those warranties? Again, you must consider your particular deal and then see if the warranties fit it. Let us assume that your represent the seller and, as in many commercial transactions, the buyer is provided with a title commitment, a plat of survey and other materials pertaining to the property and its economics and the buyer is also afforded a period of time to inspect the property, the zoning and other regulations and all relevant material. I will examine the warranties in that light. Under those assumptions, all of the "condition warranties" are suspect because the buyer is being given ample opportunity to determine the condition of the property for itself. On the other hand, I consider most of the "lease warranties" to be legitimate concerns of a buyer which may not be readily discernable by due diligent investigation. Finally, as to the "further warranties and covenants", I may have some issues with warranty (a), which is covered by the title commitment being obtained, (h) and (j), which are ascertainable from the title commitment, the survey or inquiry to the municipality, and (l), which is a remote risk in commercial properties. All of the warranties must be considered in conjunction with the provisions, if any, in the contract relating to the duration of the warranties and the remedies for breach. That will be discussed below as well.

Now let us address some examples in the lease realm. The following is some typical insurance language, which obviously is quite different from the language I include in my leases. Although the language is carefully drafted and well considered, it presents numerous issues for tenants, as we shall see. Before completing my review of the insurance provisions, however, I always ask the client to run the insurance language past its insurance agent or risk management person for comment.

For convenience, I shall interline my comments in italics:

## INSURANCE

**Tenant's Insurance. Tenant will secure and maintain, at Tenant's expense:**

**All risk property insurance (including extra expense insurance) on all of Tenant's fixtures and personal property in the Premises, and on any alterations, additions or improvements, all for the full replacement cost thereof. Tenant will use the proceeds from such insurance for the replacement of fixtures and personal property and for the restoration of any such alterations, additions, or improvements as set forth below. Landlord will be named as loss payee as respects its interest in any such alterations, additions, or other improvements.**

*"All risk insurance" is really a misnomer. No policy really insures all risks. It will be subject to specified exclusions. The actual name of the policy which insures all risk of physical loss except for the specified exclusions is called*

## Reviewing and Analyzing Documents

*"Special Form"* insurance. Note also that the tenant is required to insure alterations, additions, or improvements. The first issue is whether the tenant is required to insure the leasehold improvements made at the inception of the lease and paid for, wholly or in part by the landlord. More basically, however, I always have a problem with the entire requirement because the landlord is almost certainly required under its mortgage to insure the building with all improvements and the cost of that insurance is being paid for by the tenant in its base rent and escalations.[22] Many leases also require the tenant to show the landlord as a loss payee or additional insured on contents insurance, which this lease does not. That is not in the tenant's interest, since if there is a loss to the tenant's trade fixtures or merchandise, the check for insurance proceeds will be made payable to the landlord, or to the tenant and the landlord, which affords the landlord too much leverage against the tenant.

**Business income insurance with limits not less than Tenant's 100% gross revenue for a period of 12 months.**

*Although it is advisable for tenants to carry this insurance for their own protection, the landlord has no interest in the proceeds of this insurance, unless for some reason the rent does not abate.[23] Of course, if the landlord is carrying the property insurance on the building, it is most likely also carrying rent loss insurance, covering lost rent and pass-throughs, so it can service its debt and pay its taxes. That is also called "business income insurance", but the payee of the proceeds is the landlord, not the tenant.*

---

[22] See my article on this topic, *supra* note 11.
[23] Many leases provide that the rent does not abate if the tenant or its employees caused the casualty. This is unfair because it gives the landlord's rent insurance carrier a defense against paying insurance proceeds for which the tenant paid the premium, in its base rent or as a pass-through. The provision makes no economic sense; it is retribution only.

**Workers' compensation and employers' liability insurance.** Workers' compensation insurance in statutory limits will be provided for all employees. The employer's liability insurance will afford limits not less than $500,000 per accident, $500,000 per employee for bodily injury by disease, and $500,000 policy limit for bodily injury by disease.

> *Landlords do not have liability for worker's compensation claims. The rationale for this provision is that it protects the tenant's financial standing. Since the tenant must have this risk covered anyway, the language is not usually objected to, but the amount specified in the lease may be more than is required by law; the amount should be tied to the legal requirement.*

**Commercial general liability insurance** which insures against claims for bodily injury, personal injury, advertising injury, and property damage based upon, involving, or arising out of the use, occupancy, or maintenance of the Premises and the Project. Such insurance will afford, at a minimum, the following limits:

| | |
|---|---|
| Each Occurrence | $1,000,000 |
| General Aggregate | $2,000,000 |
| Products/Completed Operations Aggregate | $2,000,000 |
| Personal and Advertising Injury Liability | $1,000,000 |
| Fire Damage Legal Liability | $50,000 |
| Medical Payments | $5,000 |

Any general aggregate limit will apply on a per-location basis.

> *Advertising injury and products liability coverage are unusual. The amounts are not objectionable, but note the amount of the umbrella coverage required below.*

Such insurance will name Landlord, its trustees and beneficiaries, Landlord's mortgagees, Landlord's managing agent, Landlord's advisor, and their respective officers, direc-

## Reviewing and Analyzing Documents

tors, agents and employees, as additional insureds (the "Required Additional Insureds").

> *This is not unusual, but be aware that some leases require that they be named as "named insureds". That may be difficult to accomplish.*

This coverage must include blanket contractual liability, broad form property damage liability, and must contain an exception to any pollution exclusion which insures damage or injury arising out of heat, smoke, or fumes from a hostile fire. Such insurance must be written on an occurrence basis and contain a standard separation of insureds provision.

> *Make certain that the tenant has the coverage.*

Business auto liability which insures against bodily injury and property damage claims arising out of the ownership, maintenance, or use of "any auto". A minimum of a $1,000,000 combined single limit per accident will apply.

> *The landlord has no risk, so why should it be covered by this insurance?*

Umbrella excess liability insurance, on an occurrence basis, that applies excess of required commercial general liability, business auto liability, and employers liability policies, which insures against bodily injury, property damage, personal injury and advertising injury claims with the following minimum limits:

| | |
|---|---|
| Each Occurrence | $5,000,000 |
| Annual Aggregate | $5,000,000 |

These limits must be in addition to and not including those stated for underlying commercial general liability, business auto liability, and employers liability insurance. Such policy must name the Required Additional Insureds as additional insureds.

*Again, make certain that the tenant has the coverage. It is on the high side for smaller companies.*

<u>General insurance requirements</u>. All policies required to be carried by Tenant hereunder must be issued by and binding upon an insurance company licensed to do business in the state in which the property is located with a rating of at least "A-" "XII" or better as set forth in the most current issue of Best's Key Rating Guide, unless otherwise approved by Landlord. Tenant will not do or permit anything to be done that would invalidate the insurance policies required.

Liability insurance maintained by Tenant will be primary coverage without right of contribution by any similar insurance that may be maintained by Landlord.

Certificates of insurance, acceptable to Landlord, evidencing the existence and amount of each liability insurance policy required hereunder and Evidence of Property Insurance Form, Acord 27[24], evidencing property insurance as required will be delivered to Landlord prior to delivery or possession of the Premises and ten days prior to each renewal date. Certificates of insurance will include an endorsement for each policy showing that the Required Additional Insureds are included as additional insureds on liability policies (except employer's liability). The Evidence of Property Insurance Form will name Landlord as loss payee for property insurance as respects Landlord's interest in improvements and betterments. *See comment above.* Further, the certificates must include an endorsement for each policy whereby the insurer agrees not to cancel or non-renew the policy, or reduce the coverage below the limits required in this Lease, without at least 30 days' prior notice to Landlord and Landlord's managing agent, if any.

---

[24] Yes, it is spelled "Acord", and it is a certificate of insurance addressed to the landlord (in this case), but courts have held that it does not actually afford coverage to the addressee.

## Reviewing and Analyzing Documents

If Tenant fails to provide evidence of insurance required to be provided by Tenant hereunder, prior to commencement of the term and thereafter during the term, within 10 days following Landlord's request thereof, and 10 days prior to the expiration date of any such coverage, Landlord will be authorized (but not required) to procure such coverage in the amount stated with all costs thereof to be chargeable to Tenant and payable upon written invoice thereof.

The limits of insurance required by this Lease, or as carried by Tenant, will not limit the liability of Tenant or relieve Tenant of any obligation thereunder, except to the extent provided for under Paragraph 18 below (Waiver of Claims; Waiver of Subrogation). Any deductibles selected by Tenant will be the sole responsibility of Tenant.

Landlord may, at its sole discretion, change the insurance policy limits and forms which are required to be provided by Tenant; such changes will be made to conform with common insurance requirements for similar properties in similar geographic locations. Landlord will not change required insurance limits or forms more often than once per calendar year.

*This last provision is dangerous for a tenant, as it could involve the tenant in substantial additional expenses. At least this lease contains a standard, but that could be improved upon. Beware of leases which simply give the landlord the right to increase the limits in its discretion.*

<u>Landlord's Insurance</u>. Landlord agrees to maintain during the Lease Term "all-risk" insurance on the Building at replacement cost, excluding foundations and excluding the items that Tenant is required to insure as provided above.

*At least this lease requires the landlord to carry some insurance—most do not. The exclusions are objectionable, however. Foundations should be covered because if a fire occurs during the winter, the foundations could be damaged by the freezing of water used to extinguish the fire.*

> *Again, the tenant should not be required to insure its improvements or alterations, for the reasons stated above and in the article referred to in footnote 11. In addition, the landlord may carry the insurance on a replacement cost basis, but also carry it with substantial co-insurance. The landlord's policy should waive co-insurance, by having a so-called "agreed amount endorsement".*

**18. Waiver of Claims, Waiver of Subrogation.** To the extent permitted by law, Tenant waives all claims it may have against Landlord, its agents or employees for damage to property sustained by Tenant or any occupant or other person resulting from the Premises or the Project or any part of said Premises or Project becoming out of repair or resulting from any accident within or adjacent to the Premises or Project or resulting directly or indirectly from any act or omission of Landlord or any occupant of the Premises or Project or any other person while on the Premises or the Project, or resulting from any peril required to be insured against under this Lease, regardless of cause or origin. The waiver in this paragraph will also apply as to the amount of any deductible under Tenant's insurance. Particularly, but not in limitation of the foregoing sentence, all property belonging to Tenant or any occupant of the Premises that is in the Project or the Premises will be there at the risk of Tenant or other person only, and Landlord or its agents or employees will not be liable for damage to or theft of or misappropriation of such property, nor for any damage to property resulting from fire, explosion, flooding of basements or other subsurface areas, falling plaster, steam, gas, electricity, snow, water, or rain which may leak from any part of the Project or from the pipes, appliances or plumbing works therein or from the roof, street or subsurface or from any other place or resulting from dampness or any other cause whatsoever, nor for any latent defect in the Premises or in the Project. Tenant will give prompt notice to Landlord in accordance with this Lease in case of fire or accidents in the Premises or in the Project or of defects therein or in the fixtures or equipment.

## Reviewing and Analyzing Documents

*In many jurisdictions, waivers of claims against landlords for injuries to persons are unenforceable because they have been held to be against public policy. In addition, the landlord cannot rely on the tenant's waiving claims for personal injury to anyone other than the tenant who is, himself or herself, a living, breathing person.*

**Tenant agrees to include in the insurance policies which Tenant is required by this Lease to carry in accordance with [Tenant's property insurance requirement], to the fullest extent permitted by law, a waiver of subrogation against Landlord and Landlord's managing agent.**

**To the extent permitted by law, Landlord waives all claims it may have against Tenant, its agents or employees for damage to the Project resulting directly or indirectly from any act or omission of Tenant or any occupant of the Premises or any other person while on the Premises, to the extent that such claim is covered by any property insurance which Landlord is required under [Landlord's property insurance requirement] to carry on the Building. Landlord will include in any property insurance policy which Landlord may carry on the Building, to the extent permitted by law, a waiver of subrogation against Tenant.**

*This is not too bad. The phrase "is covered" should be changed to "is required to be covered" because it is possible that the landlord does not actually have the coverage required. Beware of leases which do not require the landlord to carry property insurance and which contain language which provides that the tenant is protected by the waiver of claims and the waiver of the right of subrogation only "to the extent Landlord is actually covered by valid and collectible insurance". That language places on the tenant the risks that, (1) the landlord does not have the coverage, (2) the coverage is inadequate, and (3) the proceeds are not collectible (i.e., the insurer is solvent or has some other defense to the payment of the proceeds, such as the failure of the landlord to have paid the premium). Re-*

> *member, the tenant is paying for the insurance through its rent and additional rent, and should have the benefit of it in the event of a loss, even if the loss is caused by the tenant or its employees.*

**Landlord will not be required to maintain insurance against thefts within the Premises, the Project, or any complex within which the Project is located.**

> *This is okay. That is why the tenant is carrying contents insurance.*

**Indemnification. Tenant will indemnify, defend, and hold harmless Landlord and its agents or employees against any claims or costs, including reasonable attorneys' and paralegals' fees, arising from conduct or from any breach or default on the part of Tenant, its agents or employees during the Lease Term or from such acts or conduct of any subtenant, employee, agent, servant, customer, or contractor of Tenant. In case any action or proceeding be brought against Landlord by reason of any obligation on Tenant's part to be performed under the terms of this Lease, or arising from any act or negligence of the Tenant, or of its agents or employees, Tenant upon notice from Landlord will defend the same at Tenant's expense by counsel reasonably satisfactory to Landlord.**

> *Make certain that the tenant's liability insurance policy contains "contractual liability coverage, which would insure the risk of this indemnity, to the extent that it relates to an insurable event.*

**If any damage to the Project results from any act or negligence of Tenant, Landlord may at Landlord's option repair such damage, and Tenant will thereupon pay to Landlord the total cost of such repairs and damages to the Project; provided, however, that Landlord waives any right of action against Tenant for any loss or damage to the Project, including the Premises, resulting from fire or other casualty by such act**

## Reviewing and Analyzing Documents

**or negligence if Landlord's insurance policy covers such loss or damage and permits such a waiver.**

> *Note that this language is not consistent with, and is more limited than the language above regarding the landlord's waiver of claims and the right of subrogation; for that reason, it is objectionable.*

In reviewing this insurance language, I do not intend to give a thorough lesson about insurance in commercial leases; there is still much to be learned. I have written several articles on insurance,[25] but I readily admit that my knowledge is not complete. If you know a good insurance agent who writes policies on commercial properties, you can learn much from him or her. That is how I learned what I know.

Now let us take the example of an assignment and subletting section. Again, I have interlined comments in italics.

### ASSIGNMENT AND SUBLETTING

(a) **Tenant will not assign this Lease, or any interest therein, and will not sublet the Premises, or any part thereof, or any right or privilege appurtenant thereto, or suffer any other person to occupy or use the Premises, or any portion thereof, without first requesting the consent of Landlord, in writing, not more than 120 but not less than 60 days before the effective date of such assignment or sublease.** (*The time period is far too long. Assignments and subleases are usually done on a fast-track basis, and the prospective assignee or subtenant will be long gone before 60 days has passed.*) **Any request by Tenant for Landlord's consent to a sublease or assignment must be accompanied by a copy of the proposed sublease or assignment agreement and reasonably detailed information and documentation, including current financial statements, regarding the proposed sublessee or assignee. Landlord agrees not to unrea-**

---

[25] *See supra* note 11. *See also* The Treatment of Insurable Risks in Commercial Leases, 18 REAL ESTATE REVIEW 4 (Winter 1989).

sonably withhold consent to any such assignment of this Lease or subletting of the Premises (except for any extension or expansion options or any rights of first refusal or first offer for which consent may be arbitrarily withheld), provided Tenant requests the same in writing and provided (i) at the time thereof Tenant is not in default under this Lease *(I believe that the tenant should have the opportunity to cure the default. Note that this prohibits an assignment or sublease even if the time to cure has not expired)*, **(ii) Landlord, in its sole discretion reasonably exercised, determines that the proposed use of the Premises, and the reputation, business, and financial responsibility of the proposed assignee or sublessee, are satisfactory to Landlord,** *("sole discretion" and "reasonably exercised" are inconsistent; the landlord should be reasonable)* **(iii) any assignee or sublessee expressly assumes all the obligations of this Lease on Tenant's part to be performed,** *(the sublessee does not assume the obligations under the prime lease—it is an entirely separate lease)* **(iv) such consent, if given, will not release Tenant of any of its obligations under this Lease, including without limitation, its obligation to pay rent, (v) a consent to one assignment or subletting will not be deemed to be a consent to any subsequent assignment or subletting, (vi) the proposed assignee or sublessee is not a tenant in the Building or the Project, or the subtenant or assignee of any such tenant,** *(this provision is very problematic for tenants; it is an attempt by the landlord to prevent the tenant from competing with it for tenants, but it takes away from tenants the most likely subtenants for its space; landlords seem to be very wedded to this provision, but at least it should be limited so that prospective subtenants whose needs cannot otherwise be satisfied by the landlord are permitted subtenants)* **(vii) the proposed assignee or sublessee is not a person or entity with whom Landlord or its agent is then negotiating or to or from whom Landlord or its agent has given or received any written or oral proposal within the past 12 months regarding a**

## Reviewing and Analyzing Documents

**lease of space in the Building or the Project,** *(for the same reason, landlords insist on this provision, but why should the tenant be excluded from subleasing to a prospect that is no longer in active negotiations with the landlord?)* **(viii) the proposed rental rate being charged to the sublessee or assignee is not less than that being offered by Landlord for comparable space in the Building,** *(this provision is totally objectionable since sublease rent will almost certainly be less than direct lease rent (because the tenant is eager to dispose of its space and there is a greater risk to the prospect in subleasing than in direct leasing and the rent being quoted may even be greater than the tenant is then paying under its lease); any limitation should be on Tenant's advertising the space for less, and that is covered below);* **and (ix) the proposed sublessee or assignee is not a government entity.** *(This is understandable because governmental agencies tend to be poor housekeepers or may generate more traffic than the landlord wants in its building.)*

> *Treating subleases and assignments together, as if they were essentially the same thing, is not necessarily fair. Assignments are not as common as subleases, since they are usually limited to situations where the entire space is disposed of, and are most commonly used when the tenant is selling its business, at least in that location.*

(b) **No permitted subtenant may assign or encumber its sublease or further sublease all or any portion of its subleased space, or otherwise permit the subleased space or any part of its subleased space to be used or occupied by others, without Landlord's prior written consent in each instance. Tenant may not mortgage, pledge or hypothecate its leasehold interest, and any attempted assignment, sublease or other transfer or encumbrance by Tenant in violation of the terms and covenants of this Subsection will be void.**

*From Handshake to Closing*

(c) **Neither this Lease nor any interest therein will be assignable as to the interest of Tenant by operation of law without consent of Landlord, which consent may be arbitrarily withheld.** *(This is unclear.)* **Tenant agrees that if Landlord withholds its consent to any assignment, subletting, or occupancy contrary to the provisions of this Section, Tenant's sole remedy will be to seek an injunction in equity to compel performance by Landlord to give its consent and Tenant expressly waives any right to damages for any such withholding by Landlord of its consent.** *(I would ask why this provision is part of the Subsection dealing with assignments by operation of law. In any case, a provision limiting the tenant's remedy to injunction (note that it does not even refer to a declaratory judgment action) would almost certainly have the effect of enabling the landlord to be arbitrary, since few, if any, assignees or subtenants will wait around while the parties litigate through a trial and appeals the reasonableness of the landlord's decision.)*

(d) **For purposes of this Section, any transfer of the ownership interests controlling Tenant will be deemed an assignment of this Lease unless such ownership interests are publicly traded.** *(This prevents the tenant from selling its business by selling its stock, membership or partnership interests, and there is no mechanism for consent, reasonable or otherwise, by the Landlord. It does not even deal with death transfers.)* **However, on the condition that Tenant is not in default of any term, covenant or condition of this Lease, Tenant will have the right, with advance written notice to but without the consent of Landlord, to sublease the Premises** *(why not an assignment?),* **or a portion thereof, to any corporation or entity which controls, is controlled by or is under common control with Tenant, on the condition that (y) such sublease is for a good business purpose and not principally for the purpose of avoiding Landlord's consent rights, and (z) the proposed use of the Premises and the reputation, business, and financial responsibility of the proposed**

66

## Reviewing and Analyzing Documents

sublessee are consistent with the first-class nature of the Building. The term "control" as used in this Section means a direct or indirect ownership interest with the power to directly or indirectly direct or cause the direction of the management or policies of the Tenant.

(e) In connection with each request by Tenant for Landlord's consent to a sublease or assignment, Tenant will pay to Landlord the following, regardless of whether such consent is granted or denied: an amount equal to Landlord's *(reasonable?)* out-of-pocket administrative, legal and other costs and expenses incurred in processing such request or otherwise incurred in connection with such sublease or assignment.

(f) If all or any part of the Premises are then subleased, any termination of this Lease or of Tenant's right to possession in connection with an Event of Default will, at Landlord's option, either, (a) terminate the sublease or (b) operate as an assignment to Landlord of the sublease. Landlord shall not be liable for any prepaid rents nor any security deposits paid by the subtenant. Landlord will not be liable for any other defaults of the Tenant under the sublease agreement. *(Subtenants may ask for non-disturbance agreements.)*

(g) Tenant's request for Landlord's consent to the subletting or assignment as described above will be deemed to be an offer by Tenant to sublet the Premises to Landlord for the balance of the Term upon all the same terms, covenants and conditions as are contained in this Lease or to assign this Lease to Landlord at Landlord's option. If Landlord does not accept such deemed offer in writing within 60 days after the effective date of Tenant's notice, then Landlord's right to sublease the Premises or acquire this Lease by assignment will be deemed to be waived. Alternatively, at Landlord's option, Landlord may, by giving written notice to Tenant within 60 days after the effective date of Tenant's notice, terminate this Lease with respect to the space described in Tenant's notice, as of the date specified in Tenant's notice for the commencement of the proposed assignment or sublease. However, nothing in this Subsection will be deemed to be a consent by Landlord to any subletting or assignment unless Landlord delivers to Tenant its written consent. Notwithstanding Landlord's consent on any one occasion, the right to recapture set forth in this Subsection will apply to any further subletting or assignment. *(Aside from the fact that the time period is too long, there are serious issues with this "recapture" provision. The landlord's rights could have the effect of preventing the tenant from selling its business. Further, if the tenant is proposing to sublease only a portion of its space for less than the balance of the term, and then re-occupy it for its business, it may lose the right to do so.)*

(h) **If Landlord consents to any sublease or assignment of the Premises, or any part thereof, Tenant will in consideration therefor pay to Landlord, as additional rent, 50% of the Excess Rent (defined below)** *(the landlord's rationale for this sharing is that the tenant should not profit from the landlord's risk dollars; some leases provide for more than 50% to be paid to the landlord—some even provide for 100%, which removes the incentive for the tenant to sublease or assign at a profit at all)* **after deducting from Excess Rent the reasonable and customary out-of-pocket transaction costs incurred by Tenant in connection with such subletting or assignment, including attorneys' fees, brokerage commissions, and alteration costs (which transaction costs will be amortized on a straight-line basis over the term of the sublease or assignment, as the case may be).** *(Note that many leases do not provide for the tenant's recapturing its expenses; that is unfair.)* **For purposes of this Section, "Excess Rent" means all rents, additional charges, and other consideration payable to Tenant by the subtenant or assignee for or by reason of such sublease or assignment and**

## Reviewing and Analyzing Documents

which are, in the aggregate, in excess of the rent payable under this Lease for the subleased or assigned space during the term of the sublease or assignment. *(No provision is made for excluding payments to the tenant for items which are not compensation for the occupancy of the space, such as proceeds of the sale of the tenant's business, payment for personal property or even reimbursement for the unamortized cost of tenant's improvements or alterations in the premises.)* **Any amounts payable by Tenant pursuant to this Section will be paid by Tenant to Landlord as and when amounts on account thereof are paid by any subtenant or assignee to Tenant, and Tenant agrees to promptly furnish such information with regard thereto as Landlord may request from time to time. Landlord may at any time and from time to time upon prior notice to Tenant to audit and inspect Tenant's books, records, accounts, and federal income tax returns to verify the determination of additional rent payable under this Section.**

(i) Tenant will not publicly advertise the rate for which Tenant is willing to sublet the space or assign the Lease. All public advertisements of the assignment of the Lease or sublease of the Premises, or any portion thereof, are subject to prior written approval by Landlord. The placement or display of any signs or lettering on the exterior of the Premises, or on the glass or any window or door of the Premises, or in the interior of the Premises if it is visible from the exterior, is strictly prohibited. *(I referred to this provision above.)*

(j) The listing or posting of any name, other than that of Tenant, whether on the door or exterior wall of the Premises, the Building's tenant directory in the lobby or elevator, or elsewhere, will not (a) constitute a waiver of Landlord's right to withhold consent to any sublet or assignment pursuant to this Section, (b) be deemed an implied consent by Landlord to any sublet of the Premises or any portion thereof, to any assignment or transfer of the Lease, or to any unauthorized occupancy of the Premises, except in accordance with the express terms of the Lease, or (c) operate to vest any right or interest in the Lease or in the Premises. *(I do not understand this provision; why would the landlord put another party's name on the directory if it is not consenting to the assignment or sublease?)*

(k) In the case of any assignment of this Lease by Tenant, the assignor and the assignee will be jointly and severally liable for all of the obligations of the tenant under this Lease. The joint and several liability of Tenant named herein and any immediate and remote successor in interest of Tenant (by assignment or otherwise), and the due performance of the obligations of this Lease on Tenant's part to be performed or observed, will not in any way be discharged, released or impaired by any (a) agreement which modifies any of the rights or obligations of the parties under this Lease, (b) stipulation which extends the time within which an obligation under this Lease is to be performed, (c) waiver of the performance of an obligation required under this Lease, or (d) failure to enforce any of the obligations set forth in this Lease. *(If the tenant assigns the lease, it should not continue to be liable during an extended term agreed to between the landlord and the assignee, nor for other amendments to the lease which increase the liability of the assignee.)*

To reiterate, my examples are merely to show some of the issues to be considered in reviewing and analyzing documents prepared by others and presented for review. It is my hope that the examples, in addition to teaching about a few of the substantive issues, will indicate the type of detailed review which most documents require. I will return to some of these examples later, when I discuss the negotiation of the documents.

## Reviewing and Analyzing Documents

### Matters Not Covered in the Document under Review

Of course, what is not in the document being reviewed may be as important, or more important, to your client, that what is there. Clearly, if a purchase contract is drafted by the seller, it may not have the warranties the purchaser is looking for. Loan documents may not have the right to prepay or the right to have insurance proceeds made available to the borrower to rebuild after a fire or other casualty.

Because leases generally are drafted by the landlord's attorneys and it is in the landlord's interest to blanket the issues (whereas it is in the tenant's interest to have the unfettered right to use the space as it wishes, so long as the tenant pays the rent), there is usually not much that is not covered in the lease being reviewed on behalf of the tenant. Still, there are many matters which may not be covered at all in the landlord's draft. Those matters may include the landlord's obligation to provide building security, remedies for the landlord's default, the landlord's obligation to mitigate its damages if the tenant defaults, exclusives (in the case of a shopping center lease), the tenant's rights to expand or extend, the tenant's right to grant to its lender a security interest in its personal property (and the landlord's obligation to sign an agreement with the tenant's lender, which will enable the tenant to get a loan so secured), the tenant's parking rights, agreements by the landlord to comply with laws applicable to the property as a whole, protection against service interruptions and provision for after-hours services, the tenant's rights to satellite dishes on the exterior of the building, and payment of commission to the tenant's broker. Certainly, some or all of these matters may have been the subject of the original handshake deal between the landlord and the tenant. Others may not have been considered at all.

As I mentioned above, if the lease happened to have been drafted by the tenant, it will most certainly omit matters which are important to the landlord, and the person reviewing that lease should have a copy of the landlord's standard lease in front of him or her, to see what is omitted and to respond accordingly.

I am not suggesting that the reviewing attorney use a list of items not covered to renegotiate the deal between the parties. Whether the lease being reviewed on behalf of the tenant contains

*From Handshake to Closing*

an option to extend or a right of first offer on other space in the building is really a business issue which may already have been discussed between the parties. It is appropriate for the lawyer to raise the issue with the client or the broker, but it should not be raised as an issue in the negotiations if it has already been rejected by the landlord and the client has acquiesced in that rejection.

**External Factors**
The review of the documents should not, of course, be conducted in a vacuum. Although you will have a general feeling for the transaction, and will receive input from the broker and your client, it may be essential that you be aware of certain matters outside of that information and the four corners of the document being reviewed. While a contract for the purchase of real estate may, and probably will, afford the buyer an opportunity to perform due diligence and terminate the contract if it is not satisfied with the property, is it not better to assist the client in determining, before it spends further time and money, that the property is not suitable for its purposes?

The consideration of external factors is, however, even more critical in situations, such as leases, where there is usually no due diligence period and your client, the tenant, is bound upon the execution and delivery of the lease.

If your client is leasing property for warehousing or manufacturing, there are many external issues. Landlords do not usually warrant zoning compliance, on the theory that they are unfamiliar with the tenant's use or manner of use (but more likely because they do not want the responsibility for such a warranty). You, or the client, or your client's broker, will have to check on the zoning. The client will also have to consider whether the space actually works for its purpose, if it has adequate ceiling height, sprinklers, truck docks, parking and the like. You will not generally be called upon to advise the client on those matters, provided the client understands that they are important.

If the client is leasing space in an existing office building, there is not likely to be a zoning issue or an issue as to restrictive covenants. However, there may be issues concerning other tenant's rights to lease the premises at the end of your client's term (creat-

## Reviewing and Analyzing Documents

ing a problem if your client may consider renewing its lease). Your inquiry regarding the rights of other tenants is important. Sometimes those rights are recited in recorded documents, which could create a problem if there is a misrepresentation in the lease. If your client has a medical use, there may be problems involving the adequacy of water or power, ability to conduct x-rays or other procedures which involve special construction, or even odors. Zoning or other restrictive covenants, either recorded or in other leases, may present issues, as well. You may have to raise those issues in your lease negotiation.

Retail leasing has its special questions, too, especially in a shopping center situation. What exclusive uses are reserved for other tenants? What visibility and access will the tenant have? What rights does the landlord have to modify the center or place kiosks in front of your client's store? Do the majors have the right to go dark? How fairly are the common area expenses allocated? What are the limitations on the client's use and how that may impact its ability to conduct its business or even sublet its space or assign its lease, if the business is not successful? What competing businesses are in the center or in the area of the new store? Will the location afford adequate foot traffic for the tenant's business?

In any lease, the issue of what tenant alterations may be required and whether they can actually be performed should be addressed. As I said, these types of issues must be determined before the lease is signed and the tenant is bound, and preferably during the review stage.

In the mortgage situation, external factors are not as common, but they may arise in the construction loan situation, where there are a number of conditions to the first funding which have to be satisfied. The client should be advised to carefully review the list of those conditions to be certain that they can be timely complied with, as failure to comply may delay funding and create a default under the construction contract.

**Now What?**
Assume, now, that you have finished your review and analysis, and that you have a document with your pigeon scratchings in the margin or that you have several sheets of notes. What do you do next?

What I do is raise the issues with the client or, if the client is not sophisticated in real estate matters and has a broker in which it has confidence, with that broker. Sometimes I do that in a face-to-face meeting, but more often in the form of a letter. A letter is better because it enables the client or the broker to study the issues more thoughtfully, and if the client chooses not to negotiate some issue and it later turns out to be problematic it indicates that, at least, I raised issues with the client.[26] I then review the issues with the client and/or the broker and we determine, jointly, which issues to raise with our respective counterparts.

Before proceeding, I would like to discuss three special cases. There are at least three types of real estate transactions which, in my judgment, are particularly complicated and require particular attention—conduit loans, ground leases, and subleases. These are unique because, while they are customarily negotiated between two parties, there are really three parties involved.

**Subleases**

Let us start with subleases. These are customarily negotiated between the sublandlord and the subtenant, even though they involve the rights and obligations of the prime landlord and usually require its consent. On the surface, it seems that subleases should be easy to draft and negotiate because so many of the duties of the parties are already governed by the prime lease. Often a young associate will be asked to draft a "simple" sublease pertaining to a small portion of the premises leased to the client; no one wants to spend a lot of time or money on that. But it is not as simple as it seems.

There are three traditional approaches to subleases. The first, which I will call the "all-inclusive" approach, is a full lease, often in the form of the prime lease, which deals in detail the rights and obligations of the three parties involved. While this approach is the most thorough, it is also the most detailed and time consuming. A more common approach is the "incorporation by reference" approach, in which the entire prime lease is incorporated by reference in the sublease, except for certain provisions which are expressly excluded or qualified. This approach is not so time con-

---

[26] Conversely, not raising that issue in the letter can be embarrassing, but let us assume we are thorough.

suming for the drafter, but the analyzer must carefully inspect the prime lease to see that the right sections were excluded or properly qualified. That is a detailed and time consuming project. Third, there is a "haphazard" approach, which ignores the fact that the document is a sublease. It is simple but leaves everyone wondering what the deal is.

My friend and colleague Martin Miner and I have developed a new approach, embodied in an article and a generic form published by the Real Property, Probate and Trust Section of the American Bar Association,[27] and recently revised and updated.[28] Although the concept and form are too detailed to expand upon here, suffice it to say that the idea is to write a new lease, which identifies itself as a sublease and describes the prime lease, sets out the rights and obligations of the sublandlord and the subtenant, and allocates responsibility for the performance of certain obligations based on who has ownership of the property and who has possession. If I have whetted your curiosity, read the articles and use the form—it works.

No matter what approach is used to prepare a sublease, careful consideration must be given to the terms and conditions of the prime lease, both in drafting the sublease, reviewing it, and advising the subtenant client of the terms which it must be aware of so as not to cause a default under the prime lease.

## Ground Leases

Ground leases are frequently used in some parts of the country, and infrequently used in others. They are very handy where the owner, for various reasons, wants all or a part of its property developed, but does not want to sell the land. For example, the owner may own a shopping center, and wishes to have an outlot or another portion of the center developed by another party, who will build the building and either operate the business there or sublease it to others.

---

[27] Saltz & Miner, *Subleases: A New Approach*, 34 REAL PROPERTY, PROBATE & TRUST J. 1 (Spring 1999), at 1.

[28] Saltz & Miner, *Subleases: A New Approach Revisited*, 41 REAL PROPERTY, PROBATE & TRUST J. 1 (Spring 2006), at 1.

*From Handshake to Closing*

In the ground lease situation, there are at least three and possibly more parties with an interest, even though the parties actually negotiating the deal are the ground lessor and the ground lessee. I once negotiated a ground lease on behalf of the ground lessee in which the property was a shopping center and the ground lessee was constructing a building to sublease to a movie theater operator. The ground lease and the sublease were being negotiated at the same time, and each had a material impact on the other, although it never became a three-party negotiation. There was another interested party, however, that is in the background of every ground lease, whether there is a sublease or not. It is a party whose identity may not even be known at the time of the ground lease negotiations, but whose rights are as important to the ground lessee as rights and obligations of the parties themselves. That is the potential leasehold mortgagee.

Because every lease, whether a space lease or a ground lease, creates an interest in real estate, it can theoretically be the subject matter of a mortgage. As a practical and legal matter, however, no institutional lender may lend on the security of a leasehold estate unless there is a sufficient remaining term including options, for the lender to realize the benefits of its security. Further, under a ground lease, the ground lessee almost always retains title to the fee interest in the building during the term, with the ground lessor owning only a reversion in that building. Obviously, retaining ownership of a building which cannot be severed from the underlying ground is something of a fiction, but it is an important one, particularly if there should be a taking by the exercise of the power of eminent domain. In that case, it is the owner of the fee interest in the building who will, depending on the length of the remaining term, be entitled to the lion's share of the award (which, in turn, will pay off the mortgage).

The ground lessee must, accordingly, negotiate the ground lease with a eye to the requirements of its lender, who will require the right to notice of, and an extended opportunity to cure the defaults of the ground lessee and otherwise to keep the leasehold alive and prevent its security from being wiped out as a result of defaults or bankruptcy of the ground lessee. The leasehold mortgagee will also need pretty much unfettered rights to dispose of the property to another ground lessee if it should foreclose on its mortgage, so as to have its loan paid off or to substitute a new mortgagor.

All these issues must be constantly borne in mind by both parties in connection with drafting, analyzing and negotiating ground leases.

**Conduit Mortgages**
Conduit mortgages, also known as securitized mortgages, are mortgages that are bundled together to create a security that is sold to investors. To qualify as a conduit mortgage, the documents must pass muster with an underwriter—the third party in these deals—and must also comply with certain requirements of the tax laws. For the borrower, these loans have the advantage of lower rates. However, they have numerous disadvantages. The deals are time consuming and the transaction costs are high. The servicing of the loan tends to be very rigid and prepayment can be involved and expensive. The documents tend to be voluminous and onerous, and the attorneys representing the lenders may be difficult to deal with.

Unless you are with a firm which represents conduit lenders, you are more likely to encounter conduit loans representing a borrower. In my experience, the lender's counsel like to give the impression that the underwriters give little leeway for change. However, it is critical that you review the documents as carefully as you would any other loan and that you seek to negotiate the changes which you deem important for your client. I have found that it is possible to negotiate changes which will afford considerable additional protection for your client. Although you may get a response that the underwriter will not approve certain changes you request, if you do not believe that your change really affects the security created by the documents, you should push back on those issues and you may be able to achieve some benefits. Expect a long and arduous negotiation.

**Conclusion**
These and similar deals may require substantive knowledge and experience beyond the "run-of-the-mill" leases, contracts and loan transactions which are the bread and butter of the real estate prac-

*From Handshake to Closing*

tice. Additional training and education are readily available for lawyers starting out in these transactions. Still, these are interesting deals, not to be avoided. The same general advice given in this book as to any other matters applies here as well. Preparation is still the key.

# Negotiating

## Communicating Your Response

Now we come to the fun stuff, or the nerve-wracking stuff, depending on your personality. It is in the negotiation stage that the drafter and analyzer go head-to-head to hammer out the final deal. Before we get to head-banging, however, the person reviewing the other's draft first has to communicate his or her concerns to the counterpart. There are several ways to do this, each with its advantages and disadvantages.

In simpler times, communication and negotiation often took place at the same time. Years ago I represented a landlord in negotiating shopping center leases. I would draft a lease, send it to the other side, and then get a phone call from the lawyer for the tenant saying he or she would like to meet with me. We would arrange a time and he would come over and tell me, across the desk, what changes he wanted me to make. I was just starting out at that time, so of course I had no idea what to agree to and what not to agree to. I would say that I had to take the issues up with my client and then run into my mentor's office and ask what to do. If I had been more experienced, I would have been able to settle most of the issues, leaving only certain business questions (or issues upon which we could not reach accord) for further discussions or for the clients to resolve (possibly through their brokers).

I recall representing a landlord once in connection with a major industrial lease for a flight kitchen with United Airlines. This time I went to the office in the suburbs of the tenant's in-house lawyer. The lease was for a new building and it required the tenant to replace the roof, if needed. The lawyer for United focused on that provision and said that United never undertook the roof replacement obligation; he asserted that the landlord should have the responsibility. I called to ask the client—it sounded logical to me.

*From Handshake to Closing*

The client explained to me that this was an absolute net lease and that the rent was quoted on the basis of the tenant's assuming that and numerous other risks and expenses; if the tenant wanted the landlord to undertake that responsibility, it would have to pay more rent.[29] The issue of dollars and cents made more sense than "we never do that" and ultimately United's lawyer conceded the point.

But I digress. Nowadays, the lawyers seldom meet face-to-face. Clients are simply not willing to pay the cost of their lawyer's traveling to one another's office, engaging in the inevitable small talk and negotiating the deal, which is too bad! In face-to-face negotiations, there is an entire panoply of valuable negotiation techniques that can be drawn into play that are not available if the negotiations are in an exchange of e-mails with attachments, letters, or even phone calls.

Still, if you are the reviewing attorney, you have to communicate your concerns to your counterpart and there are numerous ways to do that, with advantages and disadvantages to each. One thing you should be careful about, however, is to **make certain that your client or its broker does not send your comment letter to the other side**. Believe it or not, that often occurs, and it can have a negative impact on the negotiations, particularly if your letter contains comments or questions that are not intended to be communicated to your counterpart.

The following are four methods to communicate your comments and concerns to your counterpart:

1. You can write a letter. I like that. Pull up the letter you wrote your client (and/or the broker), re-address it to your counterpart, change the date on the header, carefully edit it to delete the questions you asked your client (or rephrase them to make your points), delete matters that your client did not deem

---

[29] The client was Milton Podolsky. He is now retired, but I have represented him and his family (Steven Podolsky is his son—*see supra* note 4) for more than 40 years. He was a broker and developer, a master negotiator, and a great teacher, and I wish to pay this tribute to him. He could sometimes get carried away, however, and give too much. Once, in an important negotiation, he gave something he should not have, and I said, "Milt, you can't give that". So he immediately said, "Well, you can't have it". He could get away with things like that.

# Negotiating

important or which he or she conceded in advance, print it, review it (always review it) and mail, fax, or e-mail it to the other lawyer. My letter usually tracks the order of the document commented up, starting with Section 1 and going to the last Section. Unfortunately, that letter may be very long and may contain such boring remarks as "in the third line of Section 6, before the word 'approved' please insert the word 'reasonably'", but those boring requests may eliminate a lot of further discussion.

2. You can mark up the document by hand and fax or PDF the marked copy to the other side. This is quick—maybe you can even send a copy of your original review version, with your marked document. It may, of course, be impossible for the drafter to read your writing or to interpret what you want.

3. If you received the document in Microsoft Word, you can save the original, create a new version, make the changes you want and send the revised document (and perhaps a comparison copy) to the drafter. Notice, of course, that by this method, you have become the drafter.

4. You can even pick up the phone and call the drafter and negotiate the points right away (or even meet with him or her).

Any of the methods of communicating you comments will get your points in front of your counterpart. I generally like Number 1, but not always. It is not confrontational; it lays out the issues without argument. It opens the door to further discussion. Of course, it does not convey much personality and, as I said, it may be boring and quite long, because it covers minor as well as major matters and deals with substantive issues as well as things like typos. If it tracks the order of the document being commented upon, it is easy for the drafter to follow, and facilitates his or her making revisions agreed to. You can also add an addendum with some language you want inserted into the document. For example, when I

*From Handshake to Closing*

am responding to an office lease draft, I usually attach a list of exclusions from operating expenses I would like included in the lease. Although I recognize the landlord's need for uniformity in its charging tenants for operating expenses, the list of exclusions is not really inconsistent with that need, because generally the landlord is not really charging the tenants for the items on the list, and even if it is, the items that are sought to be excluded are not the type operating expenses which, in my judgment, are legitimately passed on to the tenants.

## EXCLUSIONS FROM OPERATING EXPENSES

**Notwithstanding the foregoing, Operating Expenses shall not include**

- **i)** **the cost to the Landlord of any work or services performed in any instances for any tenant (including the Tenant) at the cost of such tenant;**
- **ii)** **capital expenses (except for costs of any capital improvements made or installed for the purpose of reducing Operating Expenses (and then only to the extent of such reduction in expenses) or made or installed pursuant to governmental law enacted after the date hereof, which shall be amortized in accordance with Generally Accepted Accounting Principles consistently applied);**
- **iii)** **wages, salaries, and other benefits for staff above the level of building manager;**
- **iv)** **any expense or costs associated with bringing the Property into compliance with any law, ordinance or code in effect as of the date of this Lease;**
- **v)** **the cost of any service furnished to any other occupant of the Property which Landlord does not provide to Tenant hereunder;**
- **vi)** **penalties, fines, or interest due to violations of contracts, laws, rules or regulations or due to late**

payments of taxes, utility bills or other contractual obligations;

vii) costs of environmental remediation;

viii) costs of repairs due to the negligence or intentional misconduct of Landlord or its employees, agents, or contractors;

ix) legal fees, court costs, or other fees or costs of negotiating or enforcing leases;

x) advertising and space planning expenses incurred in procuring tenants for the Property;

xi) any costs for which Landlord is reimbursed (whether by insurance or otherwise);

xii) cost of repairs, alterations, or replacements caused by casualty losses or other events to the extent actually insured or self-insured against by Landlord or required to be insured against by Landlord pursuant to this Lease;

xiii) cost of repairs, alterations, or replacements caused by the exercise of rights of condemnation or eminent domain;

xiv) fees or other compensation paid to subsidiaries or affiliates of Landlord for services on or to the Property, to the extent that the costs of such services exceed competitive costs of such services;

xv) repairs or replacements of any equipment or component of the Property caused by deficient design, selection of materials, construction or improper maintenance;

xvi) costs relating to maintaining Landlord's existence, either as a corporation, partnership, or other entity, such as trustee's fees, annual fees, partnership organization or administration expenses, business, corporation or franchise taxes, deed recordation expenses, legal and accounting fees;

*From Handshake to Closing*

    xvii) costs for purchasing and installing sculpture, paintings or other objects of art; and

    xviii) management fees in excess of three percent of gross receipts from the Property.

There is little benefit to communication method 2, except speed, and in my experience, the drafter waits as long for the response with the handwritten comments as for any other response—perhaps longer.

Method 3 has substantial benefits for the reviewer, or at least it seems to. It might just enable you, as the reviewer to take over the drafting and, in effect, become the drafter, requiring the original drafter to come back to you with his or her comments. I have done this, usually at the request of the client, and have often found that, after spending a lot more time than writing a letter would have taken,[30] the original drafter rejected this approach and dealt with the redraft as if it were merely a comment letter or worse, a handwritten mark-up.

When I am the drafter and I receive such a response, I am usually somewhat miffed. First, I am concerned that the comparison copy may not be accurate. Often that is the case, and it can be completely innocent. Sometimes revisions are made and saved on the first version and forgotten before a second version is created. I have done that myself. If I realize that I did it, I go back to the original draft and make a new copy to compare. If I fail to realize it, my comparison is wrong. That is why, when I receive a redraft, I make my own comparison, using my draft and a clean copy of the redraft. Even if I am not sent a clean copy (the re-drafter does not want to make it easy for me to re-redraft his or her draft) I can usually, but not always, do so by removing the marks from the comparison copy and creating a new clean copy. Then I run a comparison copy from the draft I submitted.

As a drafter, and one who admits to having pride of authorship, I do not want to turn the drafting over to my counterpart. Even if the redraft covers legitimate points, I have enough experience to feel that I can draft better language, more readable, clearer

---

[30] Billable hours, if you can collect for them.

# Negotiating

and, most importantly, with greater advantage for my client. So, even if I agree to make a change requested, I put it in my own document and in my own words.

More is involved here than mere pride of authorship. We are concerned here with nuance. Every drafter uses nuance to slant the document ever so slightly (or not so slightly) in his or her client's favor. Usually these nuances do not mean anything, but if there is litigation, one can never be certain where the court will focus.

## Preparation

Transmitting one's views on the draft is only the beginning of the process of reaching agreement on the terms of the document. Perhaps it is possible to reach agreement by sending drafts back and forth—certainly enough people try to do so—but ultimately, some direct communication is usually necessary to close the gaps. As I said, that direct communication can come in the form of a meeting or a telephone conversation, but whatever form it takes, it is a venture into the unexpected.

Some people are natural negotiators, who approach the event with confidence and eagerness, looking forward to the give and take. Others, and I include myself in this category, approach negotiations with a certain degree of trepidation and uncertainty. I feel that it is largely a matter of personality type.

None of us should feel that we are inexperienced at negotiation because negotiation is the way we conduct ourselves in everyday life. As children, we negotiate with our parents, grandparents, siblings, and friends; as students, with our teachers and fellow students as well as with our parents. In marriage, we negotiate with our spouses and children and, perhaps, still with our parents and siblings and certainly with our grandchildren. We negotiate with the department store's complaint department, with waiters who bring us the wrong order or err on the check. I am certain you get the idea—our lives involve repeated or continuous negotiations, yet when we sit down to negotiate the client's deal, we may feel inadequacy or even fear. Why is that?

*From Handshake to Closing*

First, we are negotiating on behalf of other people, and our decisions (and even our recommendations) have financial and other impacts on people other than ourselves. Bad advice or losing a point may have substantial, and sometimes unforeseen, consequences to the client, who will then hold us responsible. It is one thing to do a poor job negotiating on one's own behalf, but quite another to do a poor job negotiating for someone else.

Second, our counterpart may be scary. He or she may be known to us as an aggressive, no-holds-barred type of negotiator, with whom it is very unpleasant to deal. Even if the counterpart is not known to us, we may fear that he or she may be that type of person. If you are young or not very experienced, that person may be willing to take advantage of your youth or inexperience, or bully you.

Because we are all different in our feelings about and our approach to negotiation, no one can really teach a person how to negotiate generally, let alone in a particular deal. Although I have a client who tries to put words in my mouth, telling me exactly what to say in the negotiations, I cannot follow his instructions. I have to say it in my own way. That is not to say that I, or any other negotiator, can approach the negotiation without preparation, without understanding which issues are very important and which are less so, and without having some idea where the deal should turn out. The question of "where the deal should turn out" is critical. If the final result does not approximate the result required, then perhaps the deal should not be made. Although the parties had painted the agreement with a broad brush, the reviewing lawyer may realize that certain provisions of the document have economic effects which could seriously jeopardize the intended outcome, particularly if events which may or may not occur in the future, but which were not considered by the parties do, in fact, occur. For this reason, it is important for both lawyers, but particularly the lawyer who does not control the document, to prepare for the meeting or telephone conversation, and to have his or her arguments in mind.

If you are the reviewing lawyer, you have already communicated your concerns to your client (and/or its broker), you have already discussed them with your client (and/or its broker), you have determined, based on input from those people or based on

# Negotiating

your own experience, the issues for which to argue, and you have communicated with your counterpart and, perhaps, narrowed the issues to be discussed. Thus, you have a finite list of matters to be resolved in the negotiations.

If you are the drafting lawyer and have retained control of the drafting, you have other concerns. If the deal is similar to one you have negotiated several times before, you have some idea of the arguments you are likely to hear. For example, if you represent an office building in the central business district, you may have negotiated the same lease form with a large number of tenants and know what your client will agree to or not agree to. In fact, you may have a set of standard inserts to use if agreement is reached on issues you have negotiated before. The same is true if you are representing a mortgagee. On the other hand, the deal may be a one-time transaction, as to which you drafted an agreement from forms you discovered on your firm's word processing system. Then, you are pretty much in the same boat as the reviewing lawyer.

In either case, you cannot go into the negotiation without some preparation. For the reviewer, the best preparation is to review the open items, understand exactly what you are asking for, why it is significant to your client (and how significant it is) and, equally importantly (perhaps more so), why conceding the point will not be so detrimental to the other party that it should be conceded. For the lawyer having control of the document, it is equally essential that consideration be given to why the issue may be significant to the other party and what effect granting it may have on one's own client. For both lawyers, it is important to consider how various points can be compromised, so the result can be "win-win", or at least not "lose-lose". This is, after all, not a war, but an effort to negotiate a deal which will serve the interests of each party.

Unfortunately, being able to prepare takes knowledge and experience. Knowing what to press for (or what to give on), and how hard to argue involves evaluating the issue from all points of view. When the reviewer first analyzes a document, some of the notes made are based on a gut feeling—this language may, somehow, hurt my client. Even when communicating requests for revisions, that sense may continue. When it comes to arguing the point

*From Handshake to Closing*

with your counterpart, however, it is necessary to have more than a gut feeling. You must have reasons; you must be able to describe the event or condition under which the language may be harmful to your client, and you must have some idea of how to deal with the issue in a way which would not so injure the other party that your argument will be rejected.

As I said, preparation starts with the client and the client's broker if the client has one. In this regard, an experienced broker is invaluable. Feel free to pick the brain of your colleagues. It is a difficult situation, because you cannot spend so much time at your client's expense that you cease to be economical. Anyway, clients like to think that you already know everything. The same client who likes to try to put words in my mouth asks why I have to research legal issues—he says that as lawyers, we should know the law (of course, he does know better).

Let me give you an example of one of my favorite issues, and how I prepared for negotiations in a way that won the point. Many office leases require tenants to carry, at their expense, property insurance on their own improvements and alterations and to restore them in the event of a fire or other casualty. It has long been my sense that this requirement involves a double expense for the tenant because the tenant already is paying for the landlord to insure the building as improved, as part of its base rent or pass-throughs. I was negotiating a large downtown office lease on behalf of my tenant. The negotiations took place over several face-to-face meetings. At the first, I objected to the requirement that the tenant insure its alterations and improvements. The lawyer for the landlord felt that the landlord did not insure them and that the tenant had to do so, but he undertook to confirm that. At a subsequent meeting, he asserted that he had indeed confirmed that the landlord's insurance did not cover those alterations and that, accordingly, the tenant had to carry that insurance.

At that point I had an idea. I ordered a copy of the landlord's mortgage and, sure enough, the mortgage required the landlord to carry full replacement cost insurance on the building—that is, as improved. At the final negotiation meeting, I placed the mortgage on the table and asked if the landlord was violating its mortgage; I won the point.

## Negotiating

I should not gloat too much, however, because that technique did not work in negotiations with other landlords and, because the cost to the tenant of the insurance did not really make this a "deal point", I have had to concede, even though I am confident that I was correct. I had my revenge, of sorts. I wrote an article on the subject, in which I show that the landlord's requirement (which happens to be common in landlord leases) is not appropriate, either for the tenant or the landlord.[31]

Usually, however, preparation does not rise to that level. It involves reviewing the communication you made to your counterpart, rethinking the open issues and your reasons for raising them, communicating with your client's broker, if he or she is to attend the meeting or be on the conference call, and generally considering your strategy.

Knowing your counterparts or their reputation may be of assistance in planning the negotiation. If you have dealt with your counterpart before, you know what to expect. Otherwise, it may be possible to speak with others in your office and ask about the person. I recently had a phone negotiation with a lawyer who had asked her partners about me. She told me that they had spoken favorably, which was gratifying; I was glad she reported that. It also made me recognize that such an inquiry might be a useful preparation tool, especially in a major transaction. I had not realized that before.

It is very important, in connection with your preparation, to seriously consider your client's business situation. Does the client have realistic alternatives to concluding this transaction? Did the client wait too long to find a new location for its business? Is it a landlord market or a tenant market? Are there many or few other locations which would be suitable? In a mortgage situation, has the client paid a substantial commitment fee which it would lose if it did not close the loan? Is your client weak or strong financially? The same questions must be considered no matter which side you represent because answers to these questions will really determine the outcome of the negotiations. So-called "non-negotiable issues" become quite negotiable if you client has to make the deal.

---

[31] *See supra* note 6.

*From Handshake to Closing*

As a general rule, I do not ask my client to be present at the negotiations, particularly if the client is not in the real estate business, because it affords me more flexibility. Sometimes you do not want to make a decision on a matter right then and there. You may feel that you have to concede a point, but you want to give it more thought, or consider some middle ground. The ability to say that you must discuss it with your client gives you more room to consider the issue, or even the best way to concede it. Having the client there puts pressure on both you and the client to resolve the matter immediately, whether at the negotiating table or by stepping out of the meeting, and invites ill considered responses. Remember, typically it is not necessary to resolve all the issues in one meeting or one phone call. Most negotiations will take place over time, with several phone calls or meetings.

You should also consider the personality of the client to determine whether he or she should be at the negotiations. I was in a negotiation where my client and the attorney for the other party became extremely hostile and actually began calling each other unflattering names. Needless to say, I had to keep them from speaking with one another to conclude the deal.

Of course, there are exceptions to the general rule. One arises in the case when there is extreme time pressure to conclude the deal, either because the other party has alternative deals available and requires an immediate resolution on this deal, or because your own client must conclude the deal quickly or suffer substantial adverse effects. Another exception exists when the client is in the real estate business or he or she is an accomplished negotiator. But even when I have attended negotiations with those people present, it is not unusual for them to say that they have to consult with partners or other decision makers about particular issues.

**The Negotiation**

Many books have been written about the art of negotiation (and it is an art, not a science). I have not read them, so I cannot comment on their value. I learned by sitting in on negotiations when I was a young associate—a practice which seems to be submerged by the pressure to bill hours. I also learned by watching brokers or clients who happened to be excellent negotiators in action. The ability to negotiate is a personal matter, based on the negotiator's personality and style. I am aware of a few tricks, such as sitting with one's back to the window so the opponent is facing a glare, or sitting in an elevated chair to appear more powerful.

A client of mine once stood up abruptly during a negotiation, sending his chair flying, to get the full attention of the other side at the table. He claimed it was an accident and that he was going to the men's room, but whether that was true or not, he certainly did get their attention and concluded the deal.

I was at a meeting about another major deal where the broker for my client closed his notebook, said the deal was dead, and prepared to leave the meeting, all over a point important to our client but not to the other side, who then backed off.[32]

At a meeting in the office of the counterpart law firm, I turned to whisper to my client, but realized when I looked at the ceiling that we were in a room that functioned as a "whispering chamber". The people across the table could hear our whispered conference. I asked if the room was a "whispering chamber", and they sheepishly admitted it was. We then met in the hall.

I have heard, although I cannot vouch for the truth of the story, of a negotiation between Japanese and American businesspersons about a deal. The Japanese translator went to the men's room and the Americans, assuming that the Japanese businessperson did not speak English, spoke freely in front of him about the least they would accept. Needless to say, they assumed incorrectly.

There are other techniques which are considered helpful, and maybe they work for other negotiators. They include the "good cop, bad cop" approach, where two people represent one side; one is really tough on the issues and the other is conciliatory. Another is "horse trading" where a point important to one side is traded off for a point important to the other. Then there is the approach of loading a meeting with as many lawyers and businesspeople as possible to intimidate the one or two visiting negotiators represent-

---

[32] The broker, Robert Splendoria, was not kidding; he was prepared to forgo a very substantial commission and advise the client to kill a deal on which he had worked for several years, over the issue. To this day, I laud his integrity and determination to place his client's interest above his own.

*From Handshake to Closing*

ing the other side, or to require the visiting negotiators to respond to conflicting comments coming from several people.

I eschew these sorts of negotiation techniques. It is my impression that these techniques interfere with the real business of the negotiation, which is to air the issues, discuss them as dispassionately as possible, and reach a conclusion.

In a negotiation where many open issues remain, some negotiators like to start with what they consider the major points, trying to resolve them before getting into the "boilerplate" issues. There is some logic in that; if the major issues cannot be resolved, there is no point in dealing with the minor issues. I, however, do not like that approach either. From a purely mundane viewpoint, it means that it is easy to miss some issues that would be considered if one started with Section 1 and preceded to the end. It also disregards my feeling that there is no boilerplate in a lease because every provision has economic effects. A serious disadvantage of this approach is that it immediately increases the adversarial nature of the negotiation because the parties are forced to consider the most contentious issues before they have reached agreement on anything else and before they have some sense of how the negotiations are going.

Before going further, I would like to set out some "thou shalt nots".

**Never belittle your counterpart.** Statements such as, "That is ridiculous" or "That is the dumbest request I ever heard" are insulting to your counterpart who not only is offended, but is likely to become more hostile and eager to win his or her points.

**Never tell your counterpart that he or she is raising too many points.** Stating that you will consider only his or her top X number of comments may hurt the deal in the end. Remember that, as the probable drafter of the document on which your counterpart is commenting, you have created the issues that are of concern to him or her. You may be killing a viable deal or forcing another party with whom your client is making a deal into a business transaction which may be hostile and adversarial as long as it exists.

## Negotiating

**Never dismiss your counterpoint's requests.** Answers such as, "We never give that" or "Well, I never heard *that* one before" or simply "Denied, what's your next point?" belittle your counterpart, whose points should be responded to with sound argument rather than flippantly.

**Do not take advantage of your counterpart's mistakes.** More about this later.

**Do not be a "deal killer".** No matter how strongly you may feel that a deal is not in your client's best interest, it is not your decision to make. You can advise your client, tell him or her how you feel and why (always "and why"), but the decision is always the client's. It is the client's money and the client, not you, who will have to live with the consequences of the decision.

### A Scenario

Let us assume that you are representing a seller of real estate in a face-to-face negotiation. As is often the case, the purchaser prepared the contract, and you are negotiating off your counterpart's document. You have prepared yourself for the discussions, which are taking place in purchaser's lawyer's conference room. You are accompanied by your client's broker, whose input you have, but you will have to bear the laboring oar in raising points. Your counterpoint has generously provided a selection of beverages and perhaps some sweets. So far so good.

You start with some pleasantries. Perhaps you play "whom do you know?" to determine if you have acquaintances in common. That is a good ice-breaker, but do not go on too long, especially if the client is with you and is paying by the hour. It gives you a chance to show that you are really a nice person doing a job, and not a nasty, tough person. Perhaps it lets you determine something about the personality of your counterpart. This is, after all, a social interaction as well as a business one, or it should be because it allows the parties to respond more dispassionately to the issues.

It is time to get started. You take out your draft and your notes and you begin to ask for revisions in the document. As I said, I prefer to start at the beginning and go through the document in order. Some matters will be easy to resolve. Most documents have throw-away clauses that are fine if the drafter gets them, but do not trouble him or her to delete. Whether you start with Section 1 or with your major points, however, you should never start with the default section, because that gives the impression that your client considers default as a viable option.

You will certainly reach some point in the discussions when you ask for a change and the response is, "No" or even, "NO!" Here is when it is important for you to understand why the request is important to your client. On the other hand, it is also important for you to understand why your counterpart is turning you down. It would be nice if your counterpart said, "I am sorry, but I cannot give on that point because . . . ." Then you could evaluate the explanation and judge whether the reason makes sense. It also gives you the opportunity to present arguments, not only why the point is important to your client, but also why your counterpart's client will not be injured by giving the point, if that is the case. If, however, you do not get an explanation, it is perfectly appropriate for you to ask for one. Listening carefully is extremely important. Your counterpart may be more experienced or more knowledgeable than you on the point under discussion, and asking for a little lesson about the point under discussion may be useful in two ways. First and foremost, you will learn something. Whether you ultimately are convinced or not, each negotiation should afford some substantive education (I still find new ideas and new arguments for my own use in each negotiation). Second, and particularly if you are a young lawyer negotiating with an older one, you may find that his or her attitude toward you may change. He or she might become more sympathetic, less apt to bully or patronize, more apt to mentor and advise. It is even possible that your counterpart may make changes that you did not even ask for, which assist you and your client and do not hurt his or hers. I have done it. These are positive things both for you and for your client.

If, after listening to your counterpart's reasons, you determine that he or she has the better argument, and the matter is not critical to your client, you may simply agree. If you have trouble saying, "I agree with you" because it makes you feel foolish about having raised the point in the first place (I sometimes feel that way), you can simply say, "Let's move on", "I'll think about it", or "I'll talk with my client" and never raise the point again.

Milt Podolsky once told me, "If you don't have a good reason to say no, say yes. If you have a good reason, explain it. If you cannot agree, try to find a compromise position." His precept saved him a lot of money because it expedited negotiations. More importantly, however, it was good advice and enabled me to get a lot of deals done. I strongly recommend bearing this advice in mind when negotiating deals.

Needless to say, even using the Podolsky precept, you will not always reach agreement on some points. Neither lawyer should, on his or her motion, simply say, "Sorry, no deal." Here it is handy to have the broker present. You can step out of the room, discuss the matter and, possibly come up with a new compromise, or even decide to concede the point. You will lose less face conceding after discussion with a third party. You can even call your client, whom you have sequestered somewhere, to get the real decision. Bear in mind that, unless this is a "deal point" for your counterpart's client, your counterpart may be having trepidations about the firmness of his or her position, as well.

If you agree on some matters and not on others, that is okay. You can say, "Let's come back to that point", at which time it is wise to put it on a list of open items, so as not to forget it. Some negotiators talk about horse-trading—giving on some items in exchange for the other party's giving on others. I have heard it spoken of much more often than I have seen it done, for the simple reason that it usually does not work. Sure, if the cost of an issue is quantifiable, the issue can be traded for an increase or decrease in the purchase price, or in the rent. If you recall the negotiation I had with the United Airlines lawyer, which I discussed above, the landlord would have taken on the responsibility for the roof in trade for an increase in the rent. Generally, however, each issue stands on its own. What if a tenant's lawyer traded a fire and casualty issue for some unrelated one, and a fire subsequently occurred?

It is not unusual to end a meeting with a list of open items. Unless there is a special reason to conclude the deal quickly, there is nothing wrong with that. It gives each party the opportunity to evaluate what is important and what is not so important, and to consider possible compromises which were not apparent during the heat of the negotiations.

**A Lease Issue—Insurance**
I quoted above insurance sections from two different leases. A problem in negotiating these provisions is that most brokers and many real estate lawyers know little about insurance (and may really care less). Although I have recommended running the insurance impacted provisions of the lease—the clauses requiring the carrying of certain insurance, the indemnity, the waiver of subrogation, and the fire and casualty provisions—past the client's insurance agent or risk manager, I have found that on many occasions, even those people were not as sophisticated as one might expect. This means that, in your own preparation for the drafting, analyzing, and negotiation of these provisions, you must learn about it yourself. It is not difficult; there are many articles on the topic, and continuing legal education programs often offer lectures and materials on insurance.

We have, however, reached the point in this book in which we should discuss the negotiation of that issue. If you drafted a lease on behalf of the landlord using my proposed language, you likely will be confronted with the argument that the tenant should not have liability for injuries caused by the landlord's negligence, and that the landlord should indemnify the tenant against such liability. I have often been confronted with that argument myself. It has superficial appeal because it seeks to impose liability based on fault, which is an old and established concept in our law, and it argues for mutuality. What it ignores, however, is the impact of insurance. If the tenant's lawyer really tests its insurance agent or risk manager, he may well find that the allocation of risks is consistent with the insurance being carried by the tenant, or which is available by the tenant a commercially reasonable rates. In this case, the negotiation is not so much a matter of compromise, but of education.

**A Contentious Contract Issue—Warranties**
One issue that is bound to be fought over in the negotiations for a contract to the purchase real estate is that relating to the warranties

**Negotiating**

to be made by the seller. I promised a discussion of the negotiation of warranties when they were listed above. Although, as I have repeated, it is not the purpose of this book to deal with a lot of substantive issues, I feel that a discussion of each party's concerns about warranties will illustrate the negotiation process.

The warranties generating the most discussion in negotiation are those that relate to the physical condition of the property. While it is possible that the transaction is to be a quick sale in which the buyer is not afforded an opportunity to perform a due diligence inspection of the property, that situation is rare, and sellers customarily feel that, if the buyer has an ample opportunity to do its due diligence, the property should be sold "as is", with no condition warranties at all. On the other hand, the buyer may be concerned that its due diligence inspection may not turn up adverse conditions which could result in costly future repairs. What if, for example, there is a foundation leak that is not visible because of drywall, or it is not possible to determine how the air conditioning system really works because the due diligence is conducted during the winter?

A compromise negotiators frequently reach is for the parties to agree that the seller will warrant that it has received no written notice or has no knowledge of a particular adverse condition. A seller might agree to warrant, for example, that it knows of no roof leak, or that it has received no notice from any governmental body and knows of no hazardous substances on the property. The notice warranty is helpful, but the knowledge warranty may provide little comfort for the buyer. There are a number of problems with the "knowledge" solution. First of all, what type of knowledge is intended? Is it "best of knowledge", "actual knowledge", or just plain "knowledge"? What do those words or phrases imply? Are they different? What, if any, degree of investigation is required for the "best of knowledge" standard? If the seller is an individual, the buyer knows whose knowledge he or she is receiving. If the seller is an entity, is it legally bound by the actual knowledge of, say, a janitor who saw hazardous materials being dumped 25 years earlier? If an entity seller limits the knowledge warranty to specific persons, how does the buyer know it is getting someone who has access to the information? Most important, it is easier to prove that there was a building code violation, for example, than it is to prove that the person referred to in the contract had knowledge of the situation.

You can readily see that there are more question marks than periods in the paragraph about knowledge warranties. Add an "as-is, where-is" section to the contract, where the buyer concedes that it is relying on it own due diligence, and what happens to the knowledge warranties, even if that section begins, "Except as expressly warranted in this contract"? What happens if there is time limit on enforcing warranties? And why should such a time limit apply when a knowledge warranty is really a warranty that someone is not lying?

The knowledge warranty quandary is not, however, limited to condition warranties. A seller might warrant that it knows of no defaults by its tenants. That might be justifiable. However, it is not as justifiable to limit the warranty that the books and records are accurate, or that the rent roll is true and correct, the knowledge of someone. Sellers sometimes hide behind "knowledge" to limit liability as to matters that they really should know, and that cannot be relied upon without some assurance that what is shown during due diligence is not some cooked-up information.

Obviously, there are no easy answers to the warranty questions, and no easy way to negotiate a solution. Each situation is different and on each question, the parties have differing strengths and weaknesses. It is important to understand the risks, the relative bargaining positions of the parties, and the importance of the various warranties at issue, to negotiate a solution which, while never ideal, at least assists in reaching some resolution of the difficult issues involved.

Resolving the issues regarding the making of warranties and whether they should be actual warranties or knowledge warranties, however, does not dispose of the problems involved in the negotiation of warranties.

One major question to be confronted and resolved is: what is to happen if a warranty is found to be false during the conduct of due diligence, which is to say, before the closing? What if, for example, the seller warrants that the roof is in good condition, free of leaks, and the buyer's roofer or roofing consultant determines that the roof is, in fact, in poor condition and subject to leaks? Should the buyer have the right to close and sue the seller for breach of warranty? An argument to be made by the buyer's lawyer is that the buyer would not have proceeded to contract to purchase the property without the warranty, that it wants to buy the property and that it negotiated a price based on a sound roof. Language generally found in contracts taking that position state that the warranty is enforceable, irrespective of the buyer's discoveries to the contrary before the closing. The seller's lawyer's argument, on the other hand, is that the seller made the warranty in good faith (it has little reason to make a false warranty, after all) and that if it is found that the seller was mistaken, the buyer should have the right to terminate and get its earnest money back, but no other remedy. Does that have some logic? Yes, unless the seller deliberately causes the breach (and that can be dealt with by the drafters), but what about the costs the buyer incurred to find the breach, let alone for its attorneys' fees to negotiate the contract and its other due diligence? Should the seller be obligated to reimburse the buyer for those costs? Obviously, as the buyer's lawyer, you would argue for that.

All right, let us say that the breach may not be discovered before the closing, but it may occur nonetheless. Should there be some time limit on the buyer's right to proceed against the seller for the breach? The debate usually goes something like this:

**Seller's lawyer:** I want a time limit on the buyer's right to sue the seller for breach.
**Buyer's lawyer:** How about two years?
**Seller's lawyer:** Try three months.

Then the lawyers horse trade on the time, sometimes specifying different time periods for different warranties. But does really that make sense? Maybe. If the HVAC equipment stops working 18 months after the closing, is it because it was not in working order at the time the warranty was made? Or did it fail because of poor maintenance? There, a time limit does make sense. But what if the warranty is that the seller knows of no hazardous materials on the property, and he does know of them, but does not disclose them? He lied. Seven months after the closing, they are discovered, and cost a fortune to remediate. Too bad. The parties agreed that the warranty expired in six months. That, to me, is problematic.

There is also an issue of what is sometimes called the "basket", a minimum amount of damages which the buyer may claim for breaches of warranty. Obviously the seller does not want to be "nickel and dimed" with breach of warranty claims. If the rooftop HVAC unit was not in good working order, but it cost only $50 to fix it, then, the argument goes; the buyer should take that risk. So the seller's lawyer suggests that the buyer accumulate all of its claims in a "basket" at the end of the survival period, and bring a single action, but if the total claims are below a certain amount, then it is too small to be paid by the seller and the buyer should accept the risk. There is some logic in that, too (unless there are different survival periods, which gums up the concept), but what should the limit be? Should it be a dollar amount, or a percentage of the purchase price?

Thus the warranty issues do not end when the parties agree on what warranties should be made, and perhaps the issues that arise after the specific warranties are agreed to may be at least as important as the text of the warranties themselves.

**Generalizing from the Particular**

I have spent a lot of time discussing warranties, a particular issue that arises in almost every real estate sales contract. I hope it cast some light on the complexity of that issue (and that issue is particularly complex), but the real purpose was to illustrate the types of issues, and the discussions which may occur, in negotiating this and other provisions, not only of contracts, but of leases, loan documents, and other real estate documentation. It shows, I hope, the necessity of keeping one's mind focused on the effect of the provisions on the client, understanding the other party's concerns and seeking a mutually satisfactory compromise.

I use the word "compromise" advisedly. The number of questions raised and not answered in the discussion of warranties demonstrates the fluidity of the discussion and the fact that the issues are not easily resolved. Other issues in these and other documents may be more complicated, or less, but even if they appear to be less complicated and more readily solved, that outcome cannot safely be predicted. Negotiations may be brief or they may be long. The issues may be resolved in one session or on one phone call, or they may go on for many sessions. The key is to protect the client as much as possible, and to allow the client to make the ultimate decisions.

It may seem that negotiation with a sophisticated lawyer will be more protracted than with a less qualified one. In my experience, the opposite is true. I recall a negotiation regarding a complicated lease of a substantial amount of office space with a very capable lawyer. I spent many hours drafting the lease, modifying the form to meet the specifics of the deal. Several days later, my client's broker and I went to the office of the tenant's lawyer, an extremely decent man with wide experience and the highest skill. The negotiation lasted half an hour and we resolved everything. We spoke in half sentences, something like this:

**Pat:** In Section 13, I need . . .
**Sid:** Okay, you got it.
**Pat:** How about changing . . . in Section 18.
**Sid:** No, because—
**Pat:** All right, I'll pass on that.

It was not quite as brief as that, but we each knew what the other was driving at and could make decisions based on our understanding of the other lawyer's position, without extended discussion. I could yield on points that my client had yielded to before (in fact, I had standard lease inserts), and Pat understood what was important to my client and what he could not expect to get, although it did not deter his asking.

On the other hand, negotiating with an unsophisticated lawyer can be extremely problematic. Even a lawyer with ample experience in areas other than real estate may really be groping to analyze a document, may miss big issues, and raise (and sometimes dwell on) issues that are either unimportant to his or her client (but important to the other party) or matters which materially change the deal contemplated by the parties. For example, I recently negotiated a lease with a lawyer who specializes in trusts and estates. He wanted to renegotiate the business terms already agreed to by his client because he believed the costs were too high. He made his comments piecemeal and, although I made certain changes my client authorized, he came back asking for further changes even after his client had signed and delivered the lease, of which he was not aware. I felt sorry for him. Another example is the in-house corporate attorney who negotiates very few real estate deals but is expected by his superiors to be a generalist and to represent the company in all its legal matters (with the possible exception of litigation). I sometimes feel sorry for those people, too, because they are clearly qualified in their area of expertise, but not in real estate. Negotiation with them requires educating them as to the issues they raise and the effect of the provision under discussion on each of the parties.

**Mistakes**

Everyone makes mistakes. No amount of careful preparation, drafting, analysis, or discussion with one's clients and their brokers will eliminate all errors. We must do the best one can to avoid errors, and we need a lot of luck to avoid having errors cause adverse consequences for our clients and ourselves.

It may be tempting to take advantage of the errors of our counterparts. After all, our clients may be or become the beneficiary of those errors. Let me counsel strongly against that. Two of my own experiences may help me to justify that advice.

I was representing a husband who was the seller of real estate. He was in the midst of a divorce and his wife was represented by another lawyer. The wife's lawyer drafted the closing statement and, before it went to the buyer's lawyer, I noticed that the prorations had an error in favor of the seller. The buyer was purchasing subject to the existing mortgage and it was necessary to prorate the interest payable during the month of the closing. The wife's lawyer prorated based on the interest being paid in advance (with the proration being in favor of the seller), but the interest was, in fact, payable in arrears (so the proration should have favored the buyer). I called this to the wife's lawyer's attention, and his response was "Let's see if the buyer's lawyer picks this up." I was not happy with that answer, but awaited the buyer's lawyer's response. There

# Negotiating

was none. At that point, I called the wife's lawyer and told him we should correct the proration and he said, "Well, if you want to tell him about it, go ahead." I did so and the correction was made.

Whether the wife's lawyer really made a mistake or was deliberately trying to gain an advantage for his (and my) client I cannot say. What I do know is that his responses were totally inappropriate and unethical. Here was a lawyer with a fairly large and prominent firm who was selling his (and its) reputation for a few hundred dollar proration—not a good deal.

On another occasion, the error was mine. I was at a meeting with my client, the other party and the other party's lawyer. We were discussing a complicated real estate tax provision in a contract. I stated a position and my client did not respond to it. A few minutes later, my counterpart asked that we take a recess. In the hall, he took me aside and pointed out a flaw in my argument that would have cost my client a lot of money. I saw immediately the error of my argument and thanked him. We returned to the meeting and I restated our position—this time correctly.

After the meeting, I called my counterpart to thank him for correcting my error, and he said that no thank you was necessary, that I would have done the same thing for him. I like to think that, not only would I have done so, but that I would have done it in the same, discreet manner—a manner that enabled me to save face and accomplish my client's objectives.

Here the traditional golden rule really applies: "Do unto others as you would have them do unto you." Always act as if your personal integrity and reputation depend on it. They do!

## Conclusion

Negotiation is the heart of the real estate deal. It will ultimately determine the rights and obligations of the parties to the transaction. It may be conducted at a leisurely pace or under considerable time pressure. Your counterpart may be a pleasant person or a difficult one. He or she may be able, or not, experienced, or not. Your client's bargaining position may be strong, or it may be weak. All these factors, and more, will influence the outcome of the negotiation and, ultimately, the success of the transaction. There are six

*From Handshake to Closing*

things each lawyer should do to be successful in any particular negotiation: learn, learn, and learn, and prepare, prepare, and prepare.

## Finishing Up

Well, you and your counterpart have been through various negotiating sessions and have a meeting of the minds on everything. The brokers and clients have been brought into the loop and they are on board, to mix a metaphor. If the negotiations were protracted, the drafter has, most likely, been revising the document all along to incorporate the changes agreed upon and the reviewer has been examining and commenting on the changes. Are you done? Is the document ready for signature? Maybe, maybe not.

If the document is long and involved, and has gone through numerous revisions (or there are numerous documents), it is certainly not a good idea to simply rely on the fact that you have drafted or reviewed all the changes as the negotiations proceeded. It is now time to review the result, and that is important for several reasons. First, you must make certain that the final document actually does represent the agreement of the parties, as you now understand it. Most likely it does, but something may have been missed, or the drafting may have tilted the agreement in a way not intended. I am not implying deliberate manipulation, although that may happen; rather in the course of drafting, there may have been some slippage. Second, if you are the reviewer, you may see some issue that is important to your client that was missed and that was not actually discussed in the negotiations. Third, and commonly, you may find inconsistencies in the documents. A negotiated change may have been properly made in one place but not elsewhere. It may have been made in one document, but not in a related document; this is particularly common in loan documents. Those inconsistencies create ambiguity. If the same concept appears in two places and the language is different or has a slightly different emphasis or meaning, which is to govern? It is wiser to cover a matter only once, or if more than once is appropriate, the same language should be used. Fourth, it is always wise to make certain that the same nomenclature is used throughout the document. One should avoid calling a party the "tenant" in one place and the "lessee" in another; it may not have legal significance, but it looks bad. You should check to see that the drafter did not say "Tenant" when he or she meant "Landlord", or vice versa (believe me, it happens). And fifth, section cross references, the table of contents, and any glossary should be reviewed for correctness.

I can assure you that rereading documents which have been heavily negotiated can be very difficult, not to say tedious. The problem is that the reader must be extremely careful to actually read everything, not let his or her eyes or mind glance over the page with the psychological impression that it reads as it is expected to read. Perhaps a second pair of eyes may be useful, although that person may raise troublesome substantive issues after the opportunity to negotiate those changes has passed.

The final review will almost invariably raise matters which require correction. It may even require some additional negotiation, drafting, and review. Better to do it then rather than after the deal is signed, after which it may be impossible to get the corrections agreed to.

Another thing to consider is the preparation of a diary and closing checklist (if it is a deal with post execution activities). I know that these materials usually are prepared after execution, but it has occurred to me that it would be helpful to do it at this point in the process. Why? Because it is a way to see if the document really works. Can you, based on what is contained in the document, map out the timing of what must be done, and has the document covered everything that is needed for the closing? The client may not be willing to pay for it if the deal does not get signed up. But here again, it is better to know before, rather than after the deal is firm.

Okay, now the document is ready for signature. You must, of course, familiarize yourself with the execution requirements of your jurisdiction. Do you need witnesses, acknowledgments? If a party is a corporation, has the requirement for secretarial attestation and seal been abolished in your state?

Although this was mentioned before, have you confirmed that you have the correct entity? Does the entity exist? Is it in good standing? Is the party the entity with the wherewithal to perform its

## Finishing Up

obligations, or do you have a shell entity, perhaps with a similar name? Has your client reviewed the financial statements?

Although a signing ceremony might be a pleasant event, especially if there is a meal or beverage service connected with it, most often the parties will not meet to sign. They will, most likely, not even sign the same copies. The final document may even be signed electronically. Signed documents must still be delivered to be effective—putting them in the drawer will not do. Electronic delivery, such as by fax or by the e-mailing of a .pdf copy, is common. All those types of execution and delivery are legal under recent federal and state legislation. You do not need "counterpart" language, although that is common. If it is signed "by the person to be bound", the document is enforceable under the Statute of Frauds.

Congratulations! The document that you have labored over for so long and so intensely has now been signed and delivered.

# What Else?

I have deliberatively *not* asked, "What next?" Of course, in the case of a sale, the next step is almost always due diligence. The same may be true for ground leases. As I discussed above, there is due diligence for occupancy leases too, but it had better be performed before the lease is signed because most (although certainly not all) leases do not provide for a due diligence inspection between lease signing and the effective date of the lease.

Let us assume that a diary and closing checklist have been prepared. If not, it had better be prepared now.

In the case of a sale, and particularly if there are no condition warranties, the buyer will have insisted that it have a period of time to do its physical and financial inspection. If your client is a real estate developer or is otherwise in the real estate business and has experience in purchasing real estate, he or she may not need your suggestions as to how to conduct the due diligence. If, however, the purchaser is a novice in the real estate business, or is purchasing the property for its own, non-real estate business, providing your client with a good due diligence checklist will be very much appreciated. Following is one I developed.

## DUE DILIGENCE CHECKLIST

A. PHYSICAL

1. Property description including detailed description of mechanical systems
2. Plans and specifications, if available
3. Roof report
4. Engineering reports to cover the following items:
    a. Structure including the condition of the slab, columns, bumpers, structural walls, exterior doors, and dock doors
    b. Masonry
    c. Exterior caulking
    d. Exterior painting
    e. Washrooms and locker rooms
    f. Interior ventilation
    g. Unit heaters
    h. Mechanical systems including sprinkler systems, electrical, plumbing and HVAC
    i. Lighting, ceiling tiles and light lenses, dry wall, entrance steps
    j. Compliance with laws and ordinances (including ADA)
    k. Building size
    l. Parking lot
    m. Landscaping

## What Else?

5. Phase I Environmental Assessment (including asbestos)
6. Phase II Environmental Assessment, if recommended by engineer
7. Floor or space plans
8. Warranties (including roof) and assignability thereof
9. Meters in multi-tenant spaces
10. Permits
11. Soil analysis for load bearing capacity, if required
12. Access and other appurtenant rights, such as easements that benefit the property
13. Code violation search from the local municipality, if required
14. ADA compliance
15. Availability and adequacy of utilities

B. TENANT ANALYSIS (IF THERE ARE TENANTS)
 1. Financial statements and credit reports
 2. Tenant interviews covering the tenants plans regarding the building, comments regarding the building and its management, and a discussion of the business outlook of the tenant

C. ECONOMICS OF PROPERTY
 1. Analysis of historical income and expense statements
 2. Comparison of historical income and expense statements to purchaser's pro formas/budgets
 3. Cash flow analysis
 4. Review of tenant files including billing statements, tenant collections, and comparison to lease
 5. Review and analyze reimbursable and non-reimbursable expenses

D. LEASE ANALYSIS (IF THERE ARE TENANTS)
1. Review of all leases and abstract the same
2. Analyze of lease problems, if any
3. Analyze for conflicts with respect to expansion rights and option space in multiple tenant buildings
4. Analyze potential conflicts between use clauses and restrictions on retail multi-tenant properties
5. Review for options to purchase, options to terminate and rights of extension or renewal
6. Review "Go Dark" clauses and assignability clauses on multiple tenant retail properties

E. MARKET ANALYSIS
1. Rent comparable and sale comparable
2. Market descriptions/supply and demand

F. LEGAL
1. Review title commitment and exception documents
2. Review survey
3. Review zoning

G. ANCILLARY CONTRACTS
1. Insurance
2. Certificates of occupancy or equivalent
3. Management contracts to manage the property
4. Service contracts: Cancellation clause
5. Other agreements

As to the physical issues, you, as the lawyer, may become involved with the review of existing warranties, access issues, and perhaps even zoning or ADA compliance. You may also be asked to review the leases and service contracts. Title and survey issues are certainly within your bailiwick—more about that below. The main thing is that the client be aware of what must be done and how long it has to complete it.

## Title and Survey

It is critical that the lawyer, if he or she represents a buyer or a ground lessee, review the title and survey, preferably current ones. The lawyer for a tenant in an occupancy lease where the term is long or the tenant is doing costly alterations may also be well advised to review the status of the landlord's title. The custom differs from jurisdiction to jurisdiction as to which party has the obligation to pay for the title insurance or the survey. Of course, every mortgagee will require a title insurance policy insuring the priority of its lien.[33]

To evaluate the status of title and the effect of a survey it is valuable for lawyers to have some familiarity with what the policies protect against, and what they do not. To oversimplify, an owner's title insurance policy insures the owner of a piece of property that it owns marketable title to the particular parcel of property, free and clear of all encumbrances except those listed in a schedule, and that there is access to the property unless that access is limited as provided in the schedule, as well. In the case of a leasehold policy, which is now an owner's policy with a special endorsement, the policy insures that the lessor owns the property leased and that the lessee owns a valid leasehold estate in the property, subject, again, to the qualifications in a schedule. Finally, a loan policy insures that the mortgagor owns the property mortgaged and that the mortgagee has a valid lien on the property, subject, again, to the matters listed in the schedule. All the policies cover the cost of defense of the title.

One of the parties will order a title commitment, which is a commitment by the title company to issue its policy when the premium is paid. The matters listed in the schedule to the commitment are usually matters of record, and it is possible to obtain copies of the documents creating the encumbrance, so they may be examined to determine whether they have an adverse impact on the client.

---

[33] It is a felony for a title company to operate in Iowa, so in Iowa deals, the title insurance customarily is written by an out-of-state company or the parties rely on an abstract and opinion of counsel.

For example, a common encumbrance is an easement. If there is an easement for utilities five feet wide along the boundary of the property, the chances are that it will not create a problem, provided that paving a driveway over the easement area is not prohibited. On the other hand, if the property was recently a farm and the prior owner granted an easement to a pipeline company to run the pipeline diagonally across the property, or did not even specify at all where the pipeline was to run, those are problems. Of course, there may be monetary liens, litigation, or a host of other types of encumbrances raised in the schedule, which may or may not prevent your client from achieving the benefit of its bargain.

Surveys come in all shapes and sizes. There are boundary surveys, which simply show the outline of the property, so-called "spot" surveys, which show the boundaries and the building, ALTA surveys, which I will describe further below, and topographical surveys, which show the contours of the property and are needed if the property is to be graded before construction.

The ALTA survey is one prepared in accordance with the Minimum Standard Detail Requirements for ALTA/ACSM Land Title Surveys, as adopted by the American Land Title Association and The National Society of Professional Surveyors. The current standards were published in 2005.[34] The standards also include a table (Table A) of optional matters to be shown on the survey, one of which is contours. A survey prepared and certified in accordance with those standards is an excellent survey, and because the surveyor is required to examine a title commitment, it will locate and identify the various locatable encumbrances, such as easements.

When you receive copies of the survey, the title commitment and the encumbrance documents, they must all be examined, as a package, to determine if there are matters which adversely affect the value of the property for your client. If you represent a buyer, a mortgage may or may not be a problem. If it is to be paid out of the proceeds of the sale (and it permits repayment), it should not be a problem. The payment can be handled at the closing. If your client is taking subject to the mortgage, the loan documents

---

[34] The standards may be viewed at www.acsm.net/ALTA2005.pdf

## What Else?

must be reviewed and evaluated. If the loan prohibits prepayment and the buyer is intending to obtain its own financing, the transaction may not close.

Typically, the title commitment (and the title policy, when it is issued) will be have five or more standard printed exceptions. They are:

1. Rights or claims of parties in possession not shown by public records.
2. Encroachments, overlaps, boundary line disputes, or other matters which would be disclosed by an accurate survey and inspection of the Premises.
3. Easements, or claims of easements, not shown by the public records.
4. Any lien, or right to a lien, for services, labor, or material heretofore or hereafter furnished, imposed by law and not shown by the public records.
5. Taxes or special assessments that are not shown as existing liens by the public records.

It can be seen that these exceptions cover matters that the title company's review of the public records will not disclose. This does not mean that buyers, lessees, or mortgagees have to take subject to those exceptions. They customarily are waived or insured over when the seller, lessor, or mortgagor provides evidence to the title company, by affidavit, survey, letters from utilities, or other means to prove to the title company's satisfaction that it has no risk. Even if there is a risk, it may be possible to have the matter insured over if the title company is willing to take the risk or is secured against the risk, as discussed below.

If the title commitment or survey indicates problems with the property or the condition of title, such as encroachments or liens, in most jurisdictions, those problems can be dealt with to the satisfaction of the buyer, lender or tenant by obtaining endorsements to the title insurance policy which insure against loss which might result from them. The title company may be willing to assume the risk because the risk is insignificant or because the seller, borrower, or landlord is providing security to the title company to protect it from liability. Thus, if the building on the property encroaches slightly over the adjoining property, the likelihood of an action by the owner of the adjoining property is slight, and even in the event of an action, a court is not likely to order the removal of a building to satisfy the adjoining owner. In the case of a lien, such as a mechanic's lien, the title company may require the party in title to post security for anywhere from 120 to 150 percent of the amount of the lien as a condition of including an endorsement insuring over that lien. Bear in mind that the title company is not really in business to take substantial risks; its losses occur only when it makes a mistake and fails to discover some title condition.

In determining whether covering a problem by endorsement is an acceptable alternative, the party to be insured should evaluate whether having the title company pay damages for failure of a condition is an adequate remedy. If the encumbrance may materially affect the client's business, such a remedy may not be adequate, so in negotiating the contract or lease, you should protect your buyer's or lessee's right to determine whether to accept an endorsement insuring over encumbrances.

Other endorsements are often obtained, not to solve a title problem, but to afford additional protection to the buyer or mortgagee. An example of such an endorsement is the zoning endorsement, which may insure against loss if the property is not zoned as shown, or if the property does not physically comply with zoning requirements such as set-backs, adequacy of parking and the like.

If the property is improved, I usually require that the zoning endorsement affirmatively insure that the improvements are legal and conforming, which is to say that they are not non-conforming but "grandfathered" uses or conditions. Non-conforming uses or conditions can be very problematic if the period of time for compliance expires, or if a fire or casualty or major alteration negates the right to continue the non-conforming situation. Assume, for example, that a building which was built at the time the ordinance provided for a minimum 10-foot setback from the lot line but the ordinance was later amended to require a 30-foot setback in that situation. So long as the time period to conform has not expired, or a major fire has not occurred, or major modifications have not been made, the owner may continue to use the property with that setback. If one of those events occurs, however, the building would have to conform with the current ordinance. Unless a variance could be obtained, that requirement could result in the loss of a 20-foot by umpteen-foot strip of building, seriously and adversely affecting the usability of the property, its value for the owner as well as a mortgagee. I have even encountered a situation where the existing condition was neither legal nor non-conforming; in that case, I was informed that some village fathers "went to jail".

In sum, your review of the title commitment, survey, and title documents is a critical step toward assuring that your client achieves the result that you carefully drafted or reviewed, and negotiated. Even if you represent the seller, ground lessor, or borrower, you must carefully consider the matters raised by the title and survey and the issues raised by your counterpart to make certain that the other party is satisfied so that the transaction may go forward.

**Other Due Diligence Issues**
One of the matters that will certainly attract a buyer's, lender's, or tenant's attention is the environmental assessment.[35] While the study itself is performed by a qualified engineer, the results are of concern to the lawyers for the parties. Some real estate lawyers have extensive experience in environmental law while others, including this author, simply know enough to be dangerous and seek the assistance of an environmental lawyer. Not only is it important for the buyer's counsel to review the report of the engineer, it may also be important for the seller's counsel to review it while it is in a preliminary stage, before it goes to the other side. Why?

Certainly it is not appropriate for seller's counsel to seek to have his client hide any problems that may be disclosed. However, it is possible that the engineer, not having a sense about the nature of the transaction, may speculate unnecessarily or become unnecessarily passionate about problems encountered. The way the report is drafted can kill a deal both parties want to close. The environmental lawyer having experience in the type of problems raised

---

[35] For brevity's sake, I will assume for this discussion that the parties involved are a buyer and seller.

can legitimately discuss the report with the engineer to request that the report state only the facts, accurately and dispassionately.

A lawyer representing the buyer should encourage his or her client to deliver a copy of the report to him or her, so that it can be reviewed and evaluated by an attorney with the proper expertise, who can advise the buyer whether further testing is needed, whether it may have a risk of clean-up, and whether it qualifies as an "innocent purchaser" under applicable environmental laws.

If the property being purchased or mortgaged has leases, a review of the leases is important. The review of the leases can be performed by the client's management team, but often it is performed by lawyers. While the client's business people may be reviewing the leases to confirm the accuracy of a rent roll, what you, as the reviewer, are really looking for is the unusual provision. Do any leases have an option to purchase or to extend? Do they afford tenants rights to lease additional premises in the building which are already leased to other tenants? Are the rights granted in the various leases inconsistent with each other, creating the possibility of conflict later on? How different are the provisions of the leases from the standard leases that your client customarily uses, or proposes to use for this property in the future?

There may be other tasks for the lawyer, only tangentially related to the negotiation of the deal. If there is construction to be done, there may be architect and general contractor contracts to review, and construction escrows. The purchase of property may, and probably will, involve another transaction—the negotiation of loan documents. The tools you have, I hope, learned from this book can then be addressed toward the conclusion of what is, essentially, a separate transaction. Related, certainly, but separate.

## Preparing for Closing

Needless to say, once a lease is signed, there is generally no need for further involvement by the lawyers (unless a memorandum of the lease is to be prepared and recorded, but that does not involve a major effort). It is time to put it in the file and hope that there is no occasion to take it out for the purpose of dealing with a dispute. The case is different with a contract for the sale of real estate or a mortgage, and sometimes for a ground lease. In those situations, further extensive lawyer involvement is required. That involvement usually entails the assembly and preparation, and the review, of closing documents, and in particular, the closing or settlement statement (which is the roadmap of where the money is coming from and where it is going). The agreement between the parties, plus the law and customs of the jurisdiction or jurisdictions where the transaction is taking place or, more likely, where the properties are located, will govern what is required and what form the documents are to take. The diary and closing checklist prepared (hopefully) before the agreement is signed, but in any case not later than right afterwards, and constantly updated to note what has been accomplished, what prepared and what approved, will become the indispensable tool for the closers.

Preparation for closing calls for skills that are entirely different from those involved in drafting, reviewing, or negotiating documents. What is required is an ability to focus on details to see that everything needed for a successful closing is actually accomplished in time and on schedule. Still, some analysis and drafting may be required to close certain deals. I have in mind, particularly, the requirement of a third party opinion to close mortgage financing. To prepare such an opinion requires a familiarity with the loan documents so that the opining lawyer can state, subject to customary assumptions and qualifications that, among other things, the documents are enforceable in accordance with their terms. If the property is in a jurisdiction other than that of the lawyer having the principal responsibility of representing the client, or the law of a different jurisdiction is to apply, an opinion from a law firm in that jurisdiction may be required, and the documents will have to be sent to that law firm for review and the drafting and approval of its opinion. That will take time.

The preparation of a non-consolidation opinion, which may be required in the case of a conduit loan, will be even more time consuming. Briefly, that is an opinion that the pertinent facts would not warrant a bankruptcy court's consolidating the borrower with another entity and thus negating the compliance with the lender's requirement that borrower be a "single-purpose entity".[36] The drafting of such an opinion requires the use of a good current form that incorporates reference to many cases, as well as a thorough investigation and recitation of the relevant facts regarding the borrower's organization that bring the borrower within the ambit of those cases.

Another type of closing which will command considerable time and attention from the attorney for the seller is one in which the proceeds of the sale are being placed with an intermediary to allow the seller to defer the gain from the sale by means of an exchange under Section 1031 of the Internal Revenue Code. That situation can become complicated if there are a number of owners of the property being sold and if some of the owners desire to trade and others do not, or if some wish to trade for one property and others for separate property. The proper arrangements must all be made before the closing, and several additional documents will be required, some needing the signature of the buyer (I hope you provided in your contract for cooperation by the buyer in connection with the exchange).

If there are matters that cannot be resolved or items that cannot be provided before the closing, a schedule of post-closing items should be prepared and diaried, so that they are taken care of in a timely manner. If there are funds to be reserved for correction

---

[36] If an entity is a "single-purpose entity", it does not engage in any other business and is thus less likely to have other debts or file for bankruptcy.

## Preparing for Closing

of faults in the property or for other purposes, plans must be made for the creating of appropriate escrows.

As in drafting, reviewing, and negotiating, each situation is different and it is impossible, in a book such as this, to cover all those situations. My purpose is, rather, to highlight those circumstances that might arise and to alert the reader to the fact that preparation for closing is extremely detail-oriented and may be quite time consuming.

# Closing

There was not much to say about preparing for closing. There is even less to say about closing (or settlement) itself. Yes, sometimes the parties and their lawyers sit in the same room and sign and exchange documents, but that does not usually happen anymore, particularly if there has been enough time to prepare in advance of the closing. Most closings occur at the title company because the buyer wants to know it has good title to the property before the money is paid out to the seller, and because the lender wants to know that all of its conditions to funding have been satisfied and that it has an insured first lien before the loan is disbursed. Usually all the documents are signed in advance, and only the lawyers and the closer are present at the closing. Sometimes the documents are sent to the closer in advance, and neither lawyer is present; at some point, they get a phone call that the closing is over and the money is on the wire.

Being able to close efficiently is dependent, of course, on good preparation and attention to detail. If some required document has not been prepared or, if prepared, not approved by the other side or not forwarded to the closer, the entire process will be stopped, or at least slowed down. And yet, despite the best preparation, sometimes something is missing. That is why it is advisable to get the client's power of attorney which enables the lawyer to sign those missing documents on behalf of the client.

I admit that I am not a great detail person when it comes to closings. But I like to attend closings because sometimes issues arise that require smoothing out or even some further negotiations. I want to confirm that all the parties entitled to receive payment are actually being paid and, if I represent the buyer or lender, that the title insurance contains no unapproved exceptions and has the required endorsements. I also like the satisfaction of being there when everything is wrapped up and the transaction is concluded. I

*From Handshake to Closing*

prefer, however, to be there with an associate, or a paralegal, whose responsibility will be to make certain that all the required documents are on the closing table. It is a matter of what you feel comfortable with, but in any case, we do what we must to conclude the deal and satisfy the client's requirements.

# Conclusion

If you have stuck with me to this point, I congratulate you. We have zigzagged through a number of different types of deals and worked our way through the various stages of reaching their conclusion. Doing real estate deals is difficult work. There is an enormous variety of transactions and each one has its own peculiarities and difficulties. It has not been my purpose to teach you how to do lease work, loan work, or even purchase and sale work. My intent is to help you with your practice of general real estate law which, as I said at the beginning of this monograph, has become more and more complex over the years. I hope that I have, to some extent, succeeded. For me, it has been an extremely challenging and rewarding career that I hope to pursue as long as I am able.

For those of you who are just starting out in the field, and those who have been working in this vineyard for some time, I offer this advice: think for yourself. Do not feel tied to the forms you find in form books, or on your firm's computer, or even in this book. These are all aids, and sometimes pretty good ones, to the practice of real estate law. So is advice from your colleagues. But it is you and you alone who have the responsibility to give your client the best representation you can, and for that, you need to focus on the deal at hand and to make the recommendations and decisions that will enable your client to realize his or her economic goals ethically and effectively. Converting that handshake at the beginning of the deal into a heartfelt handshake at the closing is what it is all about.